MW00880249

PIT BOSS
WOOD PELLET
GRILL & SMOKER
COOKBOOK

1800 Days of Flavorful and Juicy Recipes to Wow Even the Most Experienced Pitmaster. The Complete Guide to Becoming the Undisputed BBQ Star

Joel Gordon

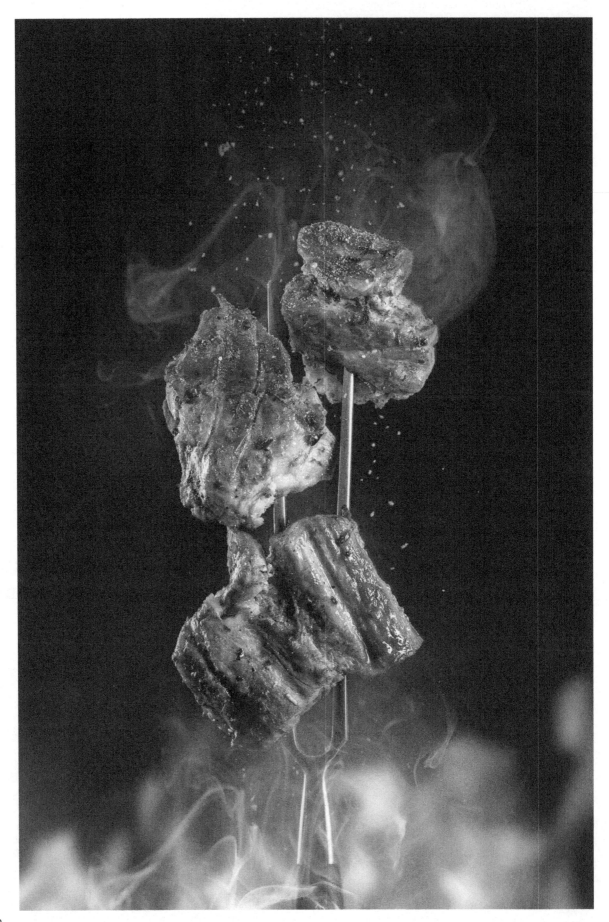

© Copyright 2022 by Joel Gordon All rights reserved.

This document is geared towards providing exact and reliable information regarding the topic and issue covered. The publication is sold with the idea that the publisher is not required to render accounting, officially permitted, or otherwise qualified services. If advice is necessary, legal or professional, a practiced individual in the profession should be ordered.

From a Declaration of Principles which was accepted and approved equally by a Committee of the American Bar Association and a Committee of Publishers and Associations.

In no way is it legal to reproduce, duplicate, or transmit any part of this document in either electronic means or in printed format. Recording of this publication is strictly prohibited and any storage of this document is not allowed unless with written permission from the publisher. All rights reserved.

The information provided herein is stated to be truthful and consistent, in that any liability, in terms of inattention or otherwise, by any usage or abuse of any policies, processes, or Instructions contained within is the solitary and utter responsibility of the recipient reader. Under no circumstances will any legal responsibility or blame be held against the publisher for any reparation, damages, or monetary loss due to the information herein, either directly or indirectly.

Respective authors own all copyrights not held by the publisher.

The information herein is offered for informational purposes solely and is universal as so. The presentation of the information is without contract or any type of guaranteed assurance.

The trademarks that are used are without any consent and the publication of the trademark is without permission or backing by the trademark owner. All trademarks and brands within this book are for clarifying purposes only and are owned by the owners themselves, not affiliated with this document.

TABLE OF CONTENTS:

INTRODUCTION

My name is Joel Gordon, and I wrote this cookbook after a lot of practice and field experience with my pit boss wood pellet grill that I purchased almost immediately after it was released. I prefer to be the first to know about breaking news. This cookbook contains practical new recipes and cooking techniques to demonstrate the difference between a regular grill and a common charcoal grill, delicious recipes that will make you the undisputed star of the evening, and simplified tables to understand what grill temperature, what pellet, and how much to cook the meat to achieve professional results. After years of having all my visitors at a BBQ at my side asking me if I could give them some guidance, I decided to put this cookbook on the market. I made the decision to reveal all my trade secrets, strategies, and directions, which result from years of expertise in the industry, to wow the visitors who follow the book to the letter.

As we go through our article, you will learn how to master your Pit Boss Wood Pellet Grill & Smoker. We also give you great recipes that we tested and perfected on this grill and smoker. This wood pellet grill is an excellent addition to your home, where you can spend quality time with family and friends. This grill is a popular addition to many people's garage or patio. It is both a smoker and a grill. As a smoker, the Pit Boss allows the home cook to smoke many foods, ranging from vegetables, fish, meat, sausage, and bacon to cheese, and nuts. As a grill, it also allows grilled favorites, such as steak and even burgers on the countertop or in the yard while still utilizing the smoking capabilities of this rugged machine.

This cookbook contains 100+ delicious recipes that can be used over a period of 1800 days, providing a wide variety of options for your daily cooking. It also will teach you all you need to know about using this fantastic gadget to improve your cooking and smoking skills. You will learn how to obtain the best results and produce the most delicious meals with ease. It is critical to understand what you are doing and how you are doing it when cooking or smoking with any type of equipment. We want all our readers to take full advantage of what this great machine offers, so it can become a staple in your household for many years to come.

Hi,

Once you have finished reading the book, hoping that the book may have been helpful and to your liking, I kindly ask that you leave an honest and dispassionate review saying what you liked or what you learned from the reading.

This will help me to disseminate this information and thus help other people like you looking for this information.

Should this book not meet your expectations, please do not hesitate to contact me at this email: gallopublishingltd@gmail.com . That way, we will have a chance to talk about it and find a solution. Also, your feedback will allow me to improve my product and ensure a better experience for the next buyer.

I sincerely thank you and wish you continued reading.

Chapter 1: KNOW YOUR MEAT CUTS

Beef

When we think of smoking and barbecue, our mind immediately goes to beef: large cuts of brisket and tri-tip, steaks over a flame. Fortunately, with today's grill technology, these are possible on a pellet grill. Selecting beef cuts is made easier by its grade. We'll go into this here, as well as some other tips to make you a master of low-and-slow meat cooking.

1. Neck-Neck will give you ribs that are moist, fall off the bone tender, and have a great beefy flavor.

2. Chuck-If you like ground beef for hamburgers, chuck is the choice. Typically, you'll find it as cubes or muscle meat. It can be fatty, but trimming it properly will make the flavor very rich. When buying, look for a chuck that has an even color with no browning (which can indicate oxidation).

3. Rib-Like chuck, this cut of beef is ground into roasts and pork roasts (which give us pork ribs). The fat will be trimmed during grinding into roasts.

4. Short Loin-Also called the ribeye, this meat is a sirloin steak. It's a thick cut of meat.

5. Sirloin-A nice-tasting piece of meat that comes from just under the hip bone. It's a pricey cut of meat but is also one of the best bets for marinating, basting, and grilling.

6. Tenderloin-Often called filet mignon, this is a cut of meat from the loin on the animal's back. It has a mild flavor and is extremely tender.

7. Round-Often cut into roasts or roasting roasts, this is a tough cut of meat. It's best served thinly sliced and trimmed of all visible fat.

8. Flank-Tender and great for making London Broil, flank punches high above its weight. Use a flavorful rub and marinade for the most flavorful flank dishes.

9. Brisket-This cut of meat punches high above its weight and is by far the most popular beef cut for BBQ and smoking. Brisket results from the breastplate of the animal. It is the fattiest of the beef cuts.

10. Top Sirloin-One of the less expensive cuts of meat, this is a cut from the upper part of the leg. It's also flavorful.

11. Rump Cap-This cut of beef is from the rump and will provide you flavor and texture. Using a rub and marinade will add to the flavor of this cut.

12. Shoulder Clod-Another great cut of beef, the clod originates from the shoulder. It's easy to prepare, so try it in your next BBQ meal.

13. Short Plate-When it is lean like a tenderloin, the short plate is great for steaks. The easiest way to trim one is to leave the flat end on for trimming and trim the wider end (known as the butt plate).

BEEF	SMOKING TIME	SMOKER TEMP.	FINAL INTERNAL TEMP.
BRISKET	12-20 Hours	225-250 F	190-200 F
BACK RIBS	4-5 Hours	225-250 F	190 F
CHUCK ROAST	12-18 Hours	225-250 F	190-200 F
PRIME RIBS	4-5 Hours	225 F	135 F
RUMP ROAST	30 Mins/Lb	225-250 F	135 F
SPARE RIBS	6-8 Hours	225-250 F	190 F
SHORT RIBS	5-6 Hours	225-250 F	190 F
TENDER LOIN	3-4 Hours	225-250 F	135 F
TRI TIP	3-4 Hours	225-250 F	135 F

Poultry

Poultry is a central part of our food culture and history. From the Thanksgiving turkey to chicken noodle soup for the common cold, poultry is everywhere. Little did you know, however, it played a large part in the spread of the pellet grill.

Think back to the first meal you had from a pellet grill. Things are changing slowly, but we would still guess 70 percent of you would say some sort of chicken. Here are some of the chicken cuts:

1. Head-Probably the best beginning cut of chicken. Because a whole chicken takes longer to cook than other types, the head is removed and saved for another time of year when a whole chicken is required for a large meal.

2. Necks-They're the best for preparing a whole chicken. The best part is that they contain little fat or blood.

3. Back-These are a few of the most flavorful pieces of meat. Tenderloin, drumsticks, feet, and back ribs are all excellent.

4. Breasts-They are usually from the inside part of the leg and are a great buy. Look for a darker, harder texture with a full layer of fat under the skin.

5. Thighs-They are from the upper part of the leg and have a higher collagen content. This makes them more fibrous.

6. Carcass-They are from the backbone of the chicken and contain a lot of connective tissue. This makes them more fibrous and hard to chew.

7. Wings-Many of us think wings are the most common cut of the bird on the BBQ. They are also great for frying, so remind yourself of this before you take them off the grill.

POULTRY	SMOKING TIME	SMOKER TEMP.	FINAL INTERNAL TEMP.
CHICKEN LEGS	1-2 Hours	275-300 F	170 F
CHICKEN THIGHS	1-2 Hours	275-300 F	170 F
CHICKEN WINGS	1-2 Hours	275-300 F	170 F
TURKEY LEGS	3-4 Hours	275-300 F	175- 180 F
WHOLE CHICKEN	2-3 Hours	275-300 F	170 F
WHOLE TURKEY	4-5 Hours	275-300 F	170 F

Pork

The meat cuts are what make pork a versatile, tasty, and affordable meat to cook with. The best way to figure out which type of cut is for you is by reading the label. If it says "pork" or "lean and tenderloin", you will be cooking a pork chop. You can also cook up sausage, bacon, or ground pork. Here are the cuts of pork meat:

1. Pork Butt (or Boston Butt)-It's a cut from the middle of the pork but, depending on the size chosen, can either be a whole or a cut. This is a whole piece of meat, not a bone-in-shoulder steak, so if you cut just a few ounces from the butt, you can feel comfortable that you'll be cooking a large piece of meat. These are usually cut into chunks for BBQ.

2. Back Ribs-These ribs come from the back of the carcass. They're normally cut into three cloves, with one of the clove's ends removed. These ribs are served without sauce.

3. St. Louis Style Ribs-These are pork back ribs cooked to perfection, so they are slow-cooked for an extended period to allow the connective tissues to break down, thus creating the perfect rib.

4. Pork Chops-These come from the loin of the hog and are some of the leanest forms of pork.

5. Cured Ham-Most of us know this cut as sausage. That's only partially true. True sausage is processed differently, so if you see sausage, it's not cured.

6. Belly-The belly is one of the fattiest cuts in pork, so in leaner cuts, it's hard to find enough fat to do the job when you're frying something.

7. Pork Tenderloin-These are lean, tender pieces of meat with the best flavor of the hog. If you taste the inside part of your arm, you will be amazed at how close the meat is to the same texture.

8. Pork Foot-This is often called the "buttock" of the animal, though even that's not 100 percent accurate. There is no "belly" to speak of. The meat is off the lower extremities of the animal, which is about the butt.

PORK	SMOKING TIME	SMOKER TEMP.	FINAL INTERNAL TEMP.
BABY BACK RIBS	5 Hours	225-250 F	180 F
BELLY BACON	6 Hours	100 F	140 F
HAM	1.5 Hours/Lb	225-250 F	160 F
LOIN	3-5 Hours	225-250 F	145 F
PORK SHOULDER	12-14 Hours	225 F	190 F
SAUSAGE	1-2 Hours	225-250 F	165 F
SPARE RIBS	6 Hours	225-250 F	180 F
TENDERLOIN	2 Hours	225-250 F	145 F

Lamb

Lamb is a light meat that originates from sheep and is available all year round. It is available in a variety of cuts, including chops, roasts, and mince.

Lamb is the most common meat in some parts of the world and can be raised on any grassland. It is also known as mutton in some countries, such as India, Italy, and Spain. Because it is easy to raise, it can be found in most parts of the world where there are sheep.

Lamb has been prized for its meat for thousands of years, but since coming to North America, lamb has only gained popularity due to its mild taste and tender texture.

Over the years, there are many ways to cook lamb, but it's best known for steaks and chops. Lamb is a great choice for grilling, broiling, roasting, and basting with a favorite sauce. It is also good for using in casseroles, stews, and soups.

Here are just some of the cuts you can get from lamb:

1. Chops - The chops cut from the shoulder of the lamb that can either be bone-in or boneless. Both chops have a T-shaped bone, but if it's bone-in, then it will have a flap of meat still attached to it while boneless chops will be sold without this flap of meat.

2. Country-Style Rib Chops - This style of lamb chop must be cut thin to melt the fat off them. They are great when slow cooked with vegetables and herbs.

3. Loin Chops - Loin chops are perfect for grilling, as they have more fat content than the chops from the shoulder. They can be much easier to prepare and cook because they contain less bone than earlier cuts.

4. Shoulder Chops - These are great for slow cooking, grilling, or barbecuing as the majority of fat has been trimmed off by butchers on the slaughter-house floor.

5. Legs & Roasts - Leg of lamb is the most popular cut you can purchase and is perfect for eating either rare or well done. It's also great for roasting in the oven, baking, and braising.

6. Shank portion - The shanks can be roasted separately; however, many people will cut them into pieces then cook them with vegetables, such as onions, carrots, and potatoes. This dish results in a lot of food that goes far and has a delicious flavor.

7. Thin Slices - These thin slices of lamb can be used in pasta dishes and other dishes that call for thin slices of meat.

8. Lamb Loin - The loin is divided into center cut, which has more fat and the smaller racks. The center cut loin has a great flavor that makes it ideal for grilling and barbecuing. This cut can also be roasted or baked in the oven; however, because it contains more fat than other cuts, you want to make sure you remove this before cooking. When cooked right, the loin will be tender and tasty!

9. Tenderloins - If you want to treat yourself, then tenderloins are the way to go. The tenderloins are the most tender kind of lamb you can get. The loin is taken from the rib portion of the animal and has very few bones, making it easy to carve.

10. Rib Racks - Rib racks come from a chest or neck section of the lamb, but they are just as lean as other cuts, and they are great for braising and slow cooking.

11. Shoulder Roasts - The shoulder roast has plenty of meat on them, so they can be cooked quickly and served whole or sliced up in other dishes.

12. Fat Loins - If you want to try something new, then try fat loins, which come from a larger shoulder portion of lamb. They are very lean and have a slightly milder taste than other cuts. They are also great for braising or slow cooking.

LAMB	SMOKING TIME	SMOKER TEMP.	FINAL INTERNAL TEMP.
LAMB LEG	4-8 Hours	225-250 F	160 F
LAMB RACK	1-2 Hours	225-250 F	145 F
LAMB SHANK	4-5 Hours	225-250 F	160 F
LAMB SHOULDER	5-6 Hours	225-250 F	160 F

Fish

A fish is typically cooked whole, so the meat consists of three main cuts: the skin (or fillet), the head, and the bone.

1. The skin or fillet is generally similar to poultry in that it may be grilled, fried, baked or broiled. It can also be prepared as a ceviche or tartar.

2. The head contains little meat but can provide other benefits to dishes where it's being used for its gelatinous qualities. For example, boiling the head of a bluefish with fresh vegetables will produce a clear broth with great jellied texture. Fish brains, heads and tails are used in many hot pot dishes. Tuna (and other fatty fish) can be cut into fillets for frying and broiling. The meat of the tuna belly is used in poke bowls and sashimi.

3. The bone from fish is a versatile ingredient. It's often used as an ingredient in soups, stews, and stir-fries, but fish bones have also been used in bone broth. In some places bone broth is a staple of cuisine while still considered a novelty at other times.

FISH	SMOKING TIME	SMOKER TEMP.	FINAL INTERNAL TEMP.
CRAB	45 Mins	225 F	145 F
LOBSTER TAILS	45 Mins	225 F	145 F
SALMON TENDER LOIN	1 Hour	220 F	145 F
SHRIMP	20-30 Mins	225 F	N/A
WHOLE SALMON	Take it Off When it Starts to Flake	220-225 F	145-150 F

Chapter 2: HOW TO TURN ON YOUR „BAD BOY"

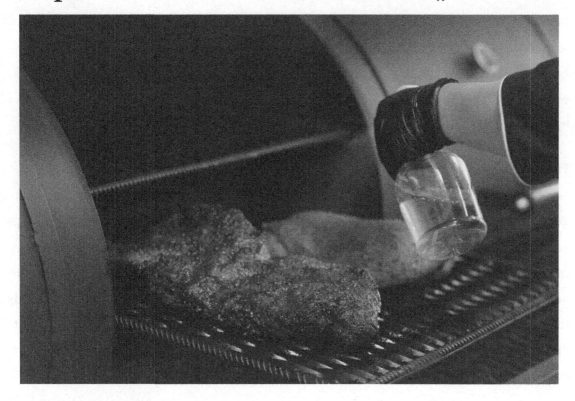

Turn on the PIT BOSS:

When using your Pit Boss Pellet grill for the first time and anytime the pellet hopper is empty, you must do the following procedures:

- Engage the PIT BOSS.
- Break the hopper open. Examine the hopper for garbage or unwelcome things.
- Remove from the grill any and all cooking components. You may discover the burn pot near the main structure's foundation.
- Simply connect the power wire to a power outlet.
- Press the power button to activate the device, and set the temperature dial to SMOKE.

Before your first usage, keep in mind the following:

- It is advisable to do a grill burn after priming the hopper and before to the first use of the grill.
- Any impurities may be eliminated by heating the grill at temperatures over 350 degrees Fahrenheit (176 degrees Celsius) for 30 to 40 minutes.

Chapter 3: THE PELLETS

Pellets, also called "wood pellets", are a non-polluting and ecological fuel. The pellet smokers usually work by combustion, the pellet will therefore be burned to produce heat in your home. Wood pellets generally come from the recycling of sawmill residues, such as sawdust and wood shavings. It is a fuel that is both efficient and economical. Wood residues, are also called **"related"**, they are dried in order to reach a favorable humidity level of less than 10%.

How do wood pellets work?

Wood pellet is in fact a fuel composed of wood chips compressed in the form of cylinders, generally small, with a diameter around 6 or 8 millimeters. The remains of different types of wood are first transformed into wood fiber, before being transported to a machine equipped with a magnet to remove all traces of metal, and then taken to a dryer. Subsequently, the wood particles are compressed to reach their final shape. These granules can be heated at high or low temperature. Different species of wood are used to make them, ranging from mesquite, hickory, apple, cherry, to pecan or even oak, for example. Thus, the possibilities as to the flavors used to cook or smoke food are numerous.

To make your favorite meal, after selecting the right kind of meat, you have to choose the right type of wood.

MEETS ⬜	BEEF	PORK	POULTRY	GAME	FISH
Wood:					
Hickory	X	X	X	X	
Apple		X	X		
Mesquite	X		X	X	X
Cherry	X	X	X	X	
Pecan	X	X	X	X	
Whiskey Barrel	X			X	X
Alder	X	X	X		X
Competition	X	X	X	X	X
Oak	X			X	X
Charcoal	X	X	X	X	
Classic	X	X	X	X	X
Fruitwood		X	X		

Chapter 4: BEEF RECIPES

Texan-Style Smoke Beef Brisket

Total Time: 15 hours & 30 minutes

Portion: 18

Recommended pellets: Black Cherry or Hickory

Ingredients:

• 1 whole packet brisket, refrigerated (14-lb, 6.3-kgs)

• Sea salt – 2 tablespoons

• Garlic powder – 2 tablespoons

• Coarsely ground black pepper – 2 tablespoons

Directions:

1. Remove the brisket from the refrigerator and flip it so the sharp edge is towards the counter. Remove and discard any silver skin or excess fat from the muscle. Between the angled and flat ends, trim the fatty part so that it is smooth. Remove and discard any extra fat or meat from the tip. Trim the apartment's corners and complete it as a square. Finally, flip the meat and slice the top to a uniform thickness of approximately half an inch (1.25 centimeters).

2. In a small bowl, combine the rub's salt, garlic powder, and pepper. Use the spice rub to fully coat the brisket.

3. The meat should be placed on the smoker so that the angled end faces the fire. Close the cover and smoke over low heat for eight hours, or until a meat thermometer registers 165 degrees Fahrenheit (74 degrees Celsius).

4. Wrap the brisket with a large piece of aluminum foil and place it in the middle of a large, clean work space. Fold the edges of the foil over the meat's edges to prevent air from entering. In the smoker, rewrap the brisket in foil, this time with the seam pointing down.

5. Lock the smoker's lid and maintain a temperature of 225 degrees Fahrenheit (110 degrees Celsius). When a thermometer placed in the middle of the brisket registers 202 degrees Fahrenheit, it is done (108 degrees Celsius). between five and eight hours have passed.

6. After cooking the meat, lay it on a cutting board and let it aside for 60 minutes before slicing.

7. Just before serving, prepare the point and flat by slicing against the grain. Serve.

Tomahawk Steak

Total Time: 2 Hours

Portion: 2 - 4

Recommended pellets: Aok

Ingredients:

- 2 salted butter buns
- 1 x 3 lb. tomahawk steak salt and pepper

Directions:

1. Before grilling the steak, ensure the meat is at ambient temperature.

2. Preheat the smoker to 220F (use Aok wood).

3. Season the beef with pepper and salt.

4. Rub and massage it.

5. Turn the meat to the grill and seal the PIT BOSS.

6. Cook the tomahawk for one hour (inside temperature should reach 118 F).

7. Take out the steak from the grill.

8. Melt butter in a cast iron skillet to sear the beef.

9. Add the steak to the hot iron skillet and sear each side for about 1-2 minutes.

10. Remove the steak at 140 F.

11. Once it has cooked, let the flank rest for 8 minutes before serving so any juices soften the beef.

Smoked Beef Ribs

Total Time: 5 to 6 hours

Portion: 4 to 8

Recommended pellets: Alder Wood Pellets

Ingredients:

- 2 (2- or 3-pound) racks beef ribs
- 2 tablespoons yellow mustard
- 1 batch Sweet & Spicy Cinnamon Rub

Directions:

1. Put wood pellets into the smoker, then turn it on. Allow the grill to reach 225 degrees Fahrenheit with the lid shut.

2. Detach the membrane from the rib cage. Using a paper towel, cut an X in the membrane and peel it away from the ribs.

3. apply mustard on the ribs and massage them. Apply the rub to the meat using your hands.

4. The ribs should be cooked on a grill to an internal temperature of between 190 and 200 degrees Fahrenheit, as measured by an instant-read thermometer.

5. After removing the rib racks from the grill, remove the individual ribs off the racks. Put it down on the table as fast as you can.

Master Tip:

Apply your chosen barbecue sauce to the ribs, then return them to the grill for another 10 minutes at 300 degrees Fahrenheit.

Smoked Roast Beef

Total Time: 12 to 14 hours

Portion: 5 to 8

Recommended pellets: Cedar, Mesquite

Ingredients:

- 1 (4-pound) top round roast
- 1 batch Espresso Brisket Rub
- 1 tablespoon butter

Directions:

1. A load of wood pellets and a turn of the smoker's crank are the first steps. Keep the grill lid closed until the temperature reaches 180 degrees.
2. The rub is applied to the top round roast. Apply the rub to the meat using your hands.
3. Smoke the roast until it reaches an internal temperature of 140 degrees Fahrenheit over direct heat from the grill. Remove the roast from the fire.
4. Place a cast-iron pan on the grill after preheating it to 450 degrees Fahrenheit and heating it to 450 degrees Fahrenheit. To cook the roast to an internal temperature of 145 degrees Fahrenheit, put it in a skillet with the butter and flip it after roughly three minutes.
5. After 10 to 15 minutes of resting after being taken from the grill, dish out the roast.

Master Tip

Substitute any beef roast you like for this recipe. As with just about every other recipe here, it is all about cooking to temperature, not time, so adjust as needed.

Smoked Burgers

Total Time: 1 hour

Portion: 4

Recommended pellets: Hickory and Teak Chips

Ingredients:

- 1 pound ground beef
- 1 egg
- Wood-Fired Burger Shake, for seasoning

Directions:

1. Prepare the smoker with wood pellets and ignite the barbecue. Keep the grill lid closed until the temperature reaches 180 degrees.
2. In a medium bowl, mix the ground beef and egg by stirring together. Make four separate patties out of the meat. Apply the burger seasoning shake to the patties to season them.
3. The next step is to smoke the burgers for 30 minutes, then serve.

4.   After increasing the grill temperature to 400 degrees Fahrenheit, continue cooking the burgers for an additional 5 minutes, or until an internal thermometer registers 145 degrees Fahrenheit. The burgers may be removed and served as desired.

Master Tip:

To add even more flavor to your burgers, dice ½ package of pellet-grilled bacon (try Apple-Smoked Bacon) and mix it into the ground beef with the egg.

BBQ Brisket

Total Time: 25 hours

Portion: 8

Recommended pellets: Kingsford Charcoal

Ingredients:

- 1 (12-14) packer beef brisket

- 1 teaspoon cayenne pepper

- 1 teaspoon cumin

- 2 tablespoons paprika

- 1 tablespoon smoked paprika

- 1 tablespoon onion powder

- ½ tablespoon maple sugar

- 2 teaspoon ground black pepper

- 2 teaspoon kosher salt

Directions:

1. In a large bowl, combine all ingredients except the brisket.

2. Wrap the beef brisket in plastic wrap and season both sides with the spice mixture. Refrigerate for a minimum of 12 hours.

3. Unwrap the brisket and let it to rest at room temperature for a minimum of two hours.

4. With the lid closed, preheat the grill to 225 degrees Fahrenheit using either mesquite or oak wood pellets.

5. Smoke the brisket for six hours on a charcoal grill. Remove the cooked brisket off the grill and cover it in aluminum foil.

6. After four hours, or when the internal temperature reaches 204 degrees Fahrenheit, return the brisket to the grill.

7. Remove the brisket from the grill and let it to stand for at least forty minutes.

8. Remove the brisket from its package and cut it into small strips.

Tri Tip Burnt Ends

Total Time: 6 hours

Portion: 2

Recommended pellets: hickory, cherry

Ingredients:

- 1/2 cup bbq sauce

- To taste, beef & brisket rub

- 1 1/2 tbsp brown sugar

- 1 1/2 tbsp butter, cubed

- 1/2 cup dr. Pepper soda

- 1/2 tbsp honey

- 2 tbsp mustard

- 2 lbs. tri tip steak

- 1/2 tbsp Worcestershire sauce

Direction:

1.   You won't need to smoke a whole brisket to savor these juicy tri tip burned ends. Santa Maria steak, or tri tip roast split, is a cut of beef that is highly marbled and has a flavorful, soft texture reminiscent of brisket. The tri tip is covered in mustard and seasoned with beef rub and brisket before being slowly smoked to provide a soft, smokey texture.

2.   Turn on the smoker, leaving the hood open for 8 minutes before setting the temperature to 225 degrees Fahrenheit.

3.   Mustard should be applied to the tri tip before the beef & brisket rub is applied.

4.   Smoke the meat for at least 2 hours and 30 minutes, or until the internal temperature reaches at least 165 degrees Fahrenheit, when cooked directly on the grill.

5.   Once the tri tip is done grilling, remove it and wrap it with pit boss butcher paper. Smoke the meat for a further two to three hours, or until the internal temperature reaches at least 200 degrees Fahrenheit, before serving.

6.   Take the tri-tip out of the oven and let it rest for 30 minutes, or put it in the fridge for the night.

7.   Turn up the grill to 275 degrees Fahrenheit.

8.   Cut the tri tip into cubes between 1/2 and 3/4 inches in size, then place in a large cast-iron frying pan.

9.   Barbecue sauce, Dr. Pepper, sugar, and Worcestershire sauce are mixed in a bowl or measuring cup, then piped over diced tri tip. Honey drops followed by brown sugar sprinkling.

10.   Smoke the pan over indirect heat on the grill. Keep the parts in the oven for 1.5–

2 hours total, turning once. The tri tip would have lost its moisture, been covered with sauce, and been scorched. Take it off the grill while it's still sizzling hot and serve it right away.

The Official Tri-tip

Total Time: 7 hours

Servings: 4

Recommended pellets: apple

Ingredients:

*   2-3 pounds beef tri-tip roast

*   ½ teaspoon garlic powder

*   1 teaspoon onion powder

*   1 teaspoon espresso powder

*   1 teaspoon brown sugar

*   1 teaspoon black pepper

*   1-1/2 teaspoon mild chili powder

*   2 teaspoons salt

Direction:

1.   Put the rub ingredients in a small dish.

2.   Place roast on a cutting board and slice up any fat cap. Score diagonal cuts on the roast surface. Turn the roast 90°and score in diamond patterns

3.   Season meat all over using the rub, making sure to press it well to coat it

4.   Place roast on the side and let it sit for 30-60 minutes

5.   Preheat your Smoker to 230°F, add wood chips to the side tray

6.   Place your tri-tip (Fat side up) on your middle rack of the Smoker. Let it smoke for 2 hours with the lid closed, until the

temperature within the grill reaches 130-135 degrees Fahrenheit.

7.   Transfer roast to a cutting board and make a tent with foil, let it sit for 20 minutes.

8.   Slice and serve

Almond Crusted Beef Fillet

Total Time: 1 hour

Servings: 4

Recommended Pellets: Pecan

Ingredients:

- 1/4 cup chopped almonds
- 1 tablespoon Dijon mustard
- 1 cup chicken broth
- Salt
- 1/3 cup chopped onion
- 1/4 cup olive oil
- Pepper
- 2 tablespoons curry powder
- 3 pounds beef fillet tenderloin

Directions:

1.   Rub the pepper and salt into the tenderloin.

2.   Place the almonds, mustard, chicken broth, curry, onion, and olive oil into a bowl. Stir well to combine.

3.   Take this mixture and rub the tenderloin generously with it.

4.   Fill the smoker with wood pellets and start. Preheat the smoker, with the hood closed, until it reaches 450°F.   .

5.   Lie on the grill, cover, and smoke for ten minutes on both sides.

6.   Continue to cook until it reaches your desired doneness.

7.   Take the entire grill and let it rest for at least ten minutes.

Beef Short Rib Lollipop

Total Time: 3 hours & 30 minutes

Servings: 4

Recommended Pellets: Hickory

Ingredients:

- 4 beef short rib lollipops
- BBQ Rub
- BBQ Sauce

Directions:

1.   Preheat your pellet grill to 275 degrees.

2.   Season all sides of the lollipop w/ the rub & place on the grill.

3.   Cook for approximately 3-4 hrs., turning regularly until the meat is tender.

4.   Baste w/ barbecue sauce during the last 30 mins., if desired.

Spicy Chuck Roast

Total Time: 5 hours

Servings: 8

Recommended Pellets: Mesquite

Ingredients:

- 2 tablespoons onion powder
- 2 tablespoons garlic powder

- 1 tablespoon red chili powder

- 1 tablespoon cayenne pepper

- Salt and ground black pepper, as required

- 1 (3-pound) beef chuck roast

- 16 fluid ounces warm beef broth

Directions:

1.	Grill temperature should be set at 250 degrees F.
2.	Combine the salt, pepper, and spices in a bowl.
3.	Apply seasoning rub liberally to chuck roast.
4.	The recommended smoking time for a roast is 3 hours total, or 1 hour and 30 minutes each side.
5.	Prepare a hot pot of beef stock and add the chuck roast.
6.	Roast for two to three hours, covered with aluminum foil.
7.	Remove the chuck roast and let it rest on a chopping board for 10 minutes.
8.	Roast must be cut before serving.

Beef Shoulder Clod

Total Time: 12-16 hours

Servings: 16-20

Recommended Pellets: Pecan

Ingredients:

- 1/2 cup sea salt

- 1/2 cup freshly ground black pepper

- 1 tablespoon red pepper flakes

- 1 tablespoon minced garlic

- 1 tablespoon cayenne pepper

- 1 tablespoon smoked paprika

- 1 (13- to 15-pound) beef shoulder clod

Directions:

1.	Combine spices
2.	Generously apply it to the beef shoulder.
3.	Fill the smoker with wood pellets and preheat to 250°F with the lid shut.
4.	Close the lid and grill the meat for 12 to 16 hours, or until an inserted thermometer reads 195 degrees Fahrenheit in the thickest portion of the steak. You may need to cover the clod with aluminum foil toward the end of smoking to prevent over-browning.
5.	Let the meat rest and serve

Smoked Rib-Eye Steaks

Total Time: 1 hour

Portion: 2

Recommended pellets: Applewood, Peach wood

Ingredients:

- 2 thick rib-eye steaks (1.5-lbs, 0.68-kgs)

- Salt and black pepper

- Steak rubs, of choice

Directions:

1.	Allow the steaks to marinade at Smoke Temperature for half an hour (room temperature).
2.	The steaks should be seasoned with salt, black pepper, and your preferred rub.

Prepare the steaks by putting them directly on the grill for around twenty minutes.

3.   The steaks should reach 400 degrees Fahrenheit (205 degrees Celsius) on the grill before being removed.

4.   On a hotter grill, steaks should be cooked for 5 minutes each side.

5.   Before serving, allow the steaks to rest for 10 minutes in foil.

6.   Cut it into pieces and serve with your preferred condiments.

Grilled Barbecue Beef Ribs

Total Time: 1 hour & 30 minutes

Portion: 4

Recommended pellets: Maple Syrup

Ingredients:

- ½ cup of Dijon mustard

- 2 tablespoons of cider vinegar

- 3 lbs. of spareribs

- 4 tablespoons of paprika powder

- ½ tablespoon of chili powder

- 1 ½ tablespoon of garlic powder

- 2 teaspoons of ground cumin

- 2 teaspoon of onion powder

- 1 ½ tablespoon of ground black pepper to taste

- 2 tablespoons of salt to taste

- 2 tablespoons of butter (optional)

Directions:

1.   Close the cover of the smoker and heat it to 350 degrees Fahrenheit with wood pellets. Combine the mustard and vinegar in a small bowl and mix them well.

2.   Coat the spareribs with the mixture and massage them with it. Blend together the paprika, chili powder, garlic powder, cumin, onion powder, salt, and pepper to taste in a second mixing bowl using a whisk until all of the ingredients are evenly distributed.

3.   Reserve a portion of the whole mixture. Season the spareribs on both sides with the remaining spice mixture.

4.   Wrap the ribs in aluminum foil, season them, and then put the butter on top to cook them (if using).

5.   To obtain an internal temperature of 165 degrees, cook the ribs on the grill for roughly one hour, flipping them periodically. Every 20 minutes, you must do a flip.

6.   When the ribs are fully cooked, remove them from the grill, remove the foil, and grill them for an additional two to five minutes, flipping them regularly, until they are nice and crispy.

7.   After a few minutes of cooling, slice and serve the ribs.

Smoked and Pulled Beef

Total Time: 6 Hours

Portion: 6

Recommended pellets: hickory

Ingredients:

- 4 lb. beef sirloin tip roast

- 1/2 cup BBQ rub

- Two bottles of amber beer

- One bottle barbecues sauce

Directions:

1.   Turn your wood pellet grill onto smoke setting then trim excess fat from the steak.

2.   Coat the steak with BBQ rub and let it smoke on the grate for 1 hour.

3.   Continue cooking and flipping the steak for the next 3 hours. Transfer the steak to a braising vessel. Add the beers.

4.   Braise the beef until tender then transfer to a platter, reserving 2 cups of cooking liquid.

5.   Use a pair of forks to shred the beef and return it to the pan. Add the reserved liquid and barbecue sauce. Stir well and keep warm before serving.

6.   Enjoy.

Teriyaki Beef Jerky

Total Time: 5 Hours & 15 minutes

Portion: 10

Recommended pellets: Hickory

Ingredients:

*   3 cups soy sauce

*   2 cups brown sugar

*   Three garlic cloves

*   2-inch ginger knob, peeled and chopped

*   1 tbsp sesame oil

*   4 lb. beef, skirt steak

Directions:

1.   Except for the meat, pulse the other ingredients in a food processor until smooth. Pulse the ingredients until smooth.

2.   Before slicing the meat into 1/4-inch thick slices, trim any visible fat. Place the steak and marinate in a plastic bag that can be sealed and refrigerate for 12 to 24 hours.

3.   Preheat for 5 minutes with the smoke mode on.

4.   Spread the steaks out on the grill and allow them to breathe. Wait 5 hours before smoking.

5.   The steak is cooked when it can be taken from the grill without difficulty and served while still warm.

Florentine Steak

Total Time: 3 hours

Portion: 2 - 4

Recommended pellets: Charcoal

Ingredients:

*   1 porterhouse steak
*   Extra virgin oil

Remark: it is very crucial that the steak is big. A perfect cut is 3 inches thick. The steak must be able to stand upright once resting on the base of the bone.

Direction:

Instructions:

1. Lightly season the beef with extra virgin olive oil.

2. Set the smoker for direct cooking and very important: use charcoal pellets.

3. Preheat to high level.

4. Once the desired temperature is reached, place the florentine on the grill diagonal to the bars.

5. Cook for 3 minutes, then move the steak to a 90-degree angle and continue cooking for another 3 minutes on the same side.

6. Turn the beef over and cook as above.

7. Now use this trick I learned in Florence.

8. Place the steak vertically with the base of the bone resting on the grill.

9. This way, heat transfers from the grill to the bone and the bone heats the inside of the steak, melting the fat inside.

10. Cook in this position for about 7 minutes.

Once it has cooked, add a pinch of coarse salt and let it rest for a few minutes before serving.

Remark: With these directions you get a medium-rare steak.

Beer Beef

Total time: 10 hours

Portion: 8 - 12

Recommended pellets: Hickory

Ingredients:

- 1 Beef Brisket 9 - 12 lbs. the fat outside trimmed

- 5 garlic cloves, smashed

- 1 onion, sliced

- 5 tablespoons Pickling Spice

- 1 tablespoon curing salt for each lb. of meat

- ½ cup Brown sugar

- 1 ½ cups Salt

- 3x12 oz. Dark beer

- 3 quarts Water, cold

- Rib seasoning

Directions:

1. In a stockpot, combine the curing salt, brown sugar, salt, beer, and water. Stir until well dissolved and add the garlic, onion, and pickling spice. Place in the fridge.

2. Add the meat to the brine but make sure it is submerged completely. Brine for 2-4 days. Stir once every day and rinse the brisket under cold water. Sprinkle with rib seasoning.

3. Preheat the grill to 250°F.

4. Cook the brisket for 4 to 5 hours. The inside grill temperature should be 160°F.

5. Wrap the meat in foil (double layer) and add water (1 ½ cup). Place it back on the grill and let it cook for 3 to 4 hours until it reaches 204°F internal grill temperature.

6. Set aside and let it sit for 30 min. Carve into thin pieces and serve. Enjoy!

Almond Crusted Beef Fillet

Total Time: 1 hour & 10 minutes

Recommended Pellets: Pecan

Portion: 4

Ingredients:

- 1/4 cup chopped almonds

- 1 tablespoon Dijon mustard

- 1 cup chicken broth

- Salt

- 1/3 cup chopped onion

- 1/4 cup olive oil

- Pepper

- 2 tablespoons curry powder

- 3 pounds beef fillet tenderloin

Directions:

1. Rub the pepper and salt into the tenderloin.

2. Place the almonds, mustard, chicken broth, curry, onion, and olive oil into a bowl. Stir well to combine.

3. Take this mixture and rub the tenderloin generously with it.

4. Fill the smoker with wood pellets and start. Preheat your smoker, with your lid closed, until it reaches 450°F.

5. Lie on the grill, cover, and smoke for ten minutes on both sides.

6. Continue to cook until it reaches your desired doneness.

7. Take the entire grill and let it rest for at least ten minutes.

Pellet Grill Meatloaf

Total Time: 6 Hours & 30 minutes

Portion: 8

Recommended pellets: apple

Ingredients:

- 1 cup breadcrumbs
- 2 pounds ground beef
- ¼ pound ground sausage
- 2 large eggs (beaten)
- 2 garlic cloves (grated)
- ½ teaspoon ground black pepper
- ¼ teaspoon red pepper flakes
- ½ teaspoon salt or to taste
- 1 teaspoon dried parsley
- 1 green onion (chopped)
- 1 teaspoon paprika
- ½ teaspoon Italian seasoning
- 1 small onion (chopped)
- 1 cup milk
- 1 cup BBQ sauce
- ½ cup apple juice

Directions:

1. Preheat the smoker to 225°F with the hood closed.

2. In a bowl, combine the egg, milk, parsley, onion, green onion, paprika, Italian seasoning, breadcrumbs, ground beef, ground sausage, salt, pepper flakes, black pepper, and garlic. Mix thoroughly until the ingredients are well combined.

3. Form the mixture into a loaf, wrap the loaf loosely in tin foil, and use a knife to poke holes in the foil. The holes will allow the smoke flavor to enter the loaf.

4. Put the wrapped loaf on the grate and grill for 1 hour 30 minutes.

5. Meanwhile, combine the BBQ sauce and apple juice in a mixing bowl.

6. Tear off the top half of the tin foil to apply the glaze. Apply the glaze over the meatloaf. Continue grilling until the internal temperature of the meatloaf is 165°F.

7. Take the meatloaf off the grill and let it stand for a few minutes.

8. Cut and serve.

Chapter 5: PORK RECIPES

St. Louis Ribs

Total Time: 2 hours & 30 minutes

Recommended pellets: Apple

Portion: 2

Ingredients:

- 1/2 cup brown sugar

- 6 tablespoons butter

- 1 cup pit boss style BBQ sauce

- To taste, pulled pork rub

- 2 St. Louis style rib racks

Directions:

1.   Start your pit boss and set the grill temperature to smoke mode with the lid open. Preheat the oven to 200° F until the fire is lit. Prepare a gas or charcoal grill for indirect fire.

2.   Remove the membrane then cut off extra fat, meat fringe, and silver skin before seasoning both sides with pulled pork rub. Place on the grill for 3 hours to smoke.

3.   Remove the ribs from the grill and position them between two sheets of pit boss butcher paper. Sprinkle with brown sugar and wrap the ribs in the butter sliced into tiny pads.

4.   Return the ribs to the grill and crank up the heat to 225° F for 2 hours. Remove the ribs then gently break open the paper with scissors, being careful not to cut into the hot steam.

5.   Fold the paper over, baste with pit boss-style sauce, and return the ribs to the barbecue (meat side up). Cook the ribs for another hour or until crispy.

6.   Remove the ribs then set aside for 15 minutes before slicing and serving sweet.

Classic Pulled Pork

Total Time: 16-20 Hours

Portion: 8-12

Recommended pellets: apple, cherry

Ingredients:

•   1 (6- to 8-pound) bone-in pork shoulder

•   2 tablespoons yellow mustard

•   1 batch Pork Rub

Directions:

1.   Prepare a fire of 225 degrees Fahrenheit in a smoker with wood pellets and a covered lid.

2.   Completely coat the pork shoulder with mustard and rub it in. Apply the rub to the meat using your hands.

3.   Smoke the shoulder until an instant-read thermometer registers 195 degrees Fahrenheit over low heat.

4.   Take the shoulder off the grill and cover it in some aluminum foil while it's still hot. Before serving, let it chill in the refrigerator for at least an hour, preferably longer.

5.   Take the pork shoulder out of the refrigerator and let it to warm up to room temperature before continuing. First remove the scapula, and then use your fingers to pull the pork from the bone. Swift preparation and service are required. It is quite possible that there will be a lot of food left over.

Pork Belly

Total Time: 4 hours and 48 minutes

Portion: 4

Recommended pellets: hickory

Ingredients:

•   5 pounds of pork belly

•   1 cup dry rub

•   3 tablespoons olive oil

For Sauce:

•   2 tablespoons honey

•   3 tablespoons butter

•   1 cup BBQ sauce

Directions:

1.   Obtain and fill a drip pan with water. Encase it with foil.

2.   Bring the temperature of your smoker to 250 degrees Fahrenheit.

3.   In a bowl, combine the pork cubes, dry rub, and olive oil.

4.   Fill the water pan halfway with water and place it on the drip pan.

5.   The side tray is in need of wood chips.

6.   Three hours of smoking pig pieces (covered).

7.   The smoked pork cubes should be taken from the smoker and mixed with honey, butter, and barbecue sauce in a foil pan.

8.   Return the pan to the smoker, cover with aluminum foil, and continue smoking for an additional 90 minutes.

9.   When the correct consistency has been attained, remove the lid and continue smoking for 15 minutes.

10.   Thus, it is served and appreciated!

Smoked Bacon

Total Time: 4 hours

Portion: 12

Recommended pellets: Hickory

Ingredients:

- Pork belly, fat trimmed – 2 pounds

- Salt – ½ cup

- Brown sugar – ½ cup

- Ground black pepper – 1 tablespoon

Directions:

1. Before preheating the grill, cure the pork and for this, stir together the ingredients for it and then rub it well on the pork belly.

2. Place pork belly into a large plastic bag, seal it, and let it rest for 8 days in the refrigerator.

3. Then remove pork belly from the refrigerator, rinse well, and pat dry.

4. When the grill has preheated, place the pork belly on the grilling rack and let smoke for 3 hours or until the control panel shows the internal temperature of 150 °F, turning halfway.

5. Check the fire after one hour of smoking and add more wood pallets if required.

6. When done, remove pork from the grill, wrap it in plastic wrap, and rest for 1 hour in the freezer until pork is firm and nearly frozen.

7. When ready to eat, cut pork into slices and then serve.

Smoked Pork Ribs

Total time: 10 hours & 20 minutes

Portion: 4

Recommended pellets: Hickory, oak

Ingredients:

- 2 rounds of baby back ribs
- 1 cup BBQ rub
- 24 ounces of apple cider
- 1 cup brown sugar
- 2 batches of BBQ sauce

Directions:

1. Prepare to smoke some wood pellets.
2. Apply barbecue sauce on the membrane of the pork ribs.
3. 5 hours in an oven warmed to 175 degrees with tobacco. Tend the grill to 225 degrees Fahrenheit.
4. In a baking dish with high sides, place meat and coat with cooking spray.
5. If you add some apple cider and sugar to the pork, it will end up having a scrumptious flavor. Wrap the pan in aluminum foil and place it back on the grill to finish cooking. Get ready to continue cooking for another four hours.
6. Place the ribs on the grill and raise the temperature to 300 degrees.
7. Barbecue sauce is applied on the ribs. The steak must now be removed from the grill and served. Enjoy.

Pork Shoulder

Total time: 36 hours

Portion: 4

Recommended pellets: Hickory

Ingredients:

• 8 pounds of pork shoulder

For the Rub:

• 1 teaspoon dry mustard

• 1 teaspoon black pepper

• 1 teaspoon cumin

• 1 teaspoon oregano

• 1 teaspoon cayenne pepper

• 1/3 cup salt

• ¼ cup garlic powder

• ½ cup paprika

• 1/3 cup brown sugar

• 2/3 cup sugar

Directions:

1. Bring your pork under salted water for 18 hours.

2. Pull the pork out from the brine and let it sit for 1 hour.

3. Rub mustard all over the pork.

4. Take a bowl and mix all rub ingredients. Rub mixture all over the meat.

5. Wrap meat and leave it overnight.

6. Take your drip pan and add water. Cover with aluminum foil. Pre-heat your smoker to 250 degrees F.

7. Use water to fill water pan halfway through and place it over drip pan. Add wood chips to the side tray.

8. Transfer meat to smoker and smoke for 6 hours.

9. Take the pork out and wrap in foil, smoke for 6 hours more at 195 degrees F.

10. Shred and serve.

11. Enjoy!

Smoked Honey - Garlic Pork Chops

Total Time: 2 hour and 15 minutes

Portion: 4

Recommended pellets: hickory

Ingredients:

• 1/4 cup of lemon juice freshly squeezed

• 1/4 cup honey (preferably a darker honey)

• 3 cloves garlic, minced

• 2 Tbsp. soy sauce (or tamari sauce)

• Salt and pepper to taste

• 24 ounces' center-cut pork chops boneless

Directions:

1. Combine honey, lemon juice, soy sauce, garlic, salt, and pepper in a bowl.

2. Cover the pork with the marinade and place it in a container.

3. Cover and marinate in the refrigerator overnight.

4. After removing pork from the marinade, dry it (save the marinade).

5. Open the lid of the pellet smoker and activate the smoke setting to start things underway. Raise the temperature to 450 degrees Fahrenheit and warm the covered pot for 10 to 15 minutes.

6. Approximately one hour after putting the meat on the grill racks, smoke it (depending on the thickness).

7. In the meanwhile, simmer the remaining marinade in a small saucepan over medium heat.

8. On a serving tray, arrange pork chops and pour marinade over them. Serve when still piping hot.

Pork Shoulder Steak

Total Time: 50 minutes

Recommended pellets: Apple

Portion: 4

INGREDIENTS:

- 4 (12 oz.) pork shoulder steaks
- 1/3 cup of olive oil
- 1 tbsp. of apple cider vinegar
- 1 tsp. of salt to taste
- 1/2 teaspoon of black pepper to taste
- One sliced onion
- 2 tbsp. of chopped parsley
- 1/2 teaspoon of chopped thyme
- 1 tsp. of ground cumin
- 1 tsp. of paprika
- 1 tsp. of oregano

Directions:

1. Start by pounding the pork to an even thickness using a meat mallet, then trim off any present fat. Put the pork inside a Ziploc bag and add other ingredients, like the oil, vinegar, onion, parsley, thyme, cumin, paprika, oregano, salt, and pepper taste, then mix/shake properly to coat. Place the pork into the refrigerator and let sit for about twenty-four hours.

2. The next step is to warm a Wood Pellet Smoker and Grill at 180 degrees Fahrenheit for fifteen minutes. Cover the container with a lid. Using aluminum foil, smoke the pork for one hour and thirty minutes. Wrap the pork in aluminum foil and continue cooking it for another 45 minutes.

3. When the pork reaches an internal temperature of 160 degrees Fahrenheit, remove the foil and return it to the grill for another 15 minutes of smoking. Before slicing and serving the pork, let it to cool for a few minutes.

Pulled Hickory-Smoked Pork Butts

Total Time: 6 hours & 45 minutes

Recommended pellets: Cherry

Portion: 20

Ingredients:

- 2 (10-pound) boneless pork butts, fresh or vacuum-packed
- 1 cup extra-virgin olive oil flavored with roasted garlic
- ¾ cup Pork Dry Rub, Jan's Original Dry Rub, or your favorite pork dry rub

Directions:

1. As you see fit, remove the fat cap and any big bits of surplus fat from the pork butt.

2.	Double-wrap the grilled pork butts in sturdy aluminum foil. While you double-wrap the packages, keep the meat probes in the butts.

3.	Rewrap the pork butts and set them at 350 degrees Fahrenheit on the Pit Boss smoker-grill.

4.	The pork butts wrapped in foil must be roasted to an internal temperature of 200 to 205 degrees.

5.	The pig butts are braised for three to 4 hours, then pulled and served.

6.	To shred the smoked pork butts, using a pulling motion. Heat-resistant gloves enable me to utilize my hands with more ease.

7.	If desired, the jerked pork butts may be mixed with any leftover juices.

8.	The grilled pork should be served on a fresh bun with coleslaw, mayonnaise, cheese, and horseradish, among other condiments

Wet-Rubbed St. Louis Ribs

Total Time: 4 hours

Portion: 3

Recommended pellets: oak pecan

Ingredients:

- 1/2 cup brown sugar
- 1 tablespoon cumin.
- 1 tablespoon ancho chili
- 1 tablespoon smoked paprika
- 1 tablespoon garlic salt
- 3 tablespoons balsamic vinegar
- 1 Rack St. Louis style ribs
- 2 cups apple juice

Directions:

1.	Except for the ribs, add the other ingredients to a mixing bowl and toss to incorporate. After applying the rub to both sides of the ribcage, let them 10 minutes to rest.

2.	Preheat the smoker for 15 minutes at 180 degrees Fahrenheit. Two hours of smoking the ribs.

3.	Cook the ribs and apple juice in foil at 250 degrees Fahrenheit.

4.	Smoke the pork for a further two hours after returning it to the grate.

5.	Before serving, remove it from the heat and let it rest for 5 minutes. Enjoy.

Maplewood Bourbon BBQ Ham

Total time: 2 hours & 45 minutes

Recommended pellets: Cherry

Portion: 8

Ingredients:

- 1 large ham
- 1/2 cup brown sugar
- 3 tbsp. bourbon
- 2 tbsp. lemon
- 2 tbsp. Dijon mustard
- ¼ cup apple juice
- ¼ cup maple syrup
- 1 tsp salt
- 1 tsp freshly ground garlic
- 1 tsp ground black pepper

Directions:

1.	Put the grill on a smoke setting.

2.   Replace the grill's cover and increase the temperature to 325 degrees.

3.   Ham wrapped in aluminum foil and placed on the smoker rack. For an internal temperature of 125 degrees Fahrenheit, smoke the ham for two hours.

4.   Stir together the sugar, bourbon, lemon juice, mustard, apple juice, salt, pepper, and maple over medium to high heat.

5.   Start with high heat to bring the ingredients to a boil, then reduce to a simmer and cook for about 10 minutes, or until the sauce thickens.

6.   Apply a glaze of maple syrup on the ham.

7.   Smoke at 370 degrees Fahrenheit until the internal temperature of the ham reaches 140 degrees.

8.   Remove the glazed ham from the grill and allow it to absorb the glaze for about 15 minutes.

9.   Ham served in bite-sized bits.

Pork Sirloin Tip Roast

Total Time: 1½ to 3 hours

Servings: 4 to 6

Recommended pellets: Hickory

Ingredients:

•   Pit Boss: Apple, Hickory

•   Apple-injected Roasted Pork Sirloin Tip Roast

•   1 (1½ to 2 pounds) pork sirloin tip roast

•   ¾ cup 100% apple juice

•   2 tablespoons roasted garlic–seasoned extra-virgin olive oil

•   5 tablespoons Pork Dry Rub or a business rub, for example, Plowboys BBQ Bovine Bold

Directions:

1.   Dry the roast with a piece of paper

2.   Utilize a flavor/marinade injector to infuse all zones of tip roast with the apple juice.

3.   Rub the whole roast with the olive oil and afterward cover generously with the rub.

4.   Utilize 2 silicone nourishment grade cooking groups or butcher's twine to support the roast.

5.   Roast the meat until the internal grill temperature arrives at 145°F, about 1½ hours.

6.   Rest the roast under a free foil tent for 15 minutes.

7.   Remove the cooking groups or twine and cut the roast contrary to what would be expected.

Double-Smoked Ham

Total Time: 2½ to 3 ½ hours

Recommended pellets: Hickory

Servings: 8 to 12

Ingredients:

•   1 (10-pound) applewood-smoked, boneless, wholly cooked, ready-to-eat ham or bone-in smoked ham

Directions:

1.   Remove the ham from its bundling and let sit at room grill temperature for 30 minutes.

2.   Arrange the Pit Boss smoker-grill for a non-direct cooking and preheat to 180°F utilizing apple or hickory Pit Boss relying upon what sort of wood was utilized for the underlying smoking.

3.   Place the ham directly on the grate and cook the ham for 1 hour at 180°F.

4.   After 60 minutes, increase pit grill temperature to 350°F.

5.   Cooking Time the ham until the internal grill temperature arrives at 140°F, about 1½ to 2 additional hours.

6.   Remove the ham and wrap in foil for 15 minutes before cutting contrary to what would be expected.

Florentine Ribeye Pork Loin

Total Time: 90 minutes

Servings: 6 to 8

Recommended pellets: Pecan

Ingredients:

- 1 (3-pound) boneless ribeye pork loin roast

- 4 tablespoons extra-virgin olive oil, divided

- 2 tablespoons Pork Dry Rub or your favorite pork seasoning

- 4 bacon slices

- 6 cups fresh spinach

- 1 small red onion, diced

- 6 cloves garlic, cut into thin slivers

- ¾ cup shredded mozzarella cheese

Directions:

1.   Trim away any abundance fat and silver skin.

2.   Butterfly the pork loin or approach your butcher to butterfly it for you. There are numerous phenomenal recordings online with nitty gritty directions on the various systems for butterflying a loin roast.

3.   Rub 2 tablespoons of the olive oil on each side of the butterflied roast and season the two sides with the rub.

4.   In a skillet cook the bacon. Disintegrate and set aside. Reserve the bacon fat.

5.   Grill the pork loin for 60 to 75 minutes, or until the internal temperature arrives at 140°F.

6.   Rest the pork loin under a free foil tent for 15 minutes before cutting contrary to what would be expected.

Buttermilk Pork Sirloin Roast

Total Time: 4 hours

Servings: 4 to 6

Recommended pellets: Apple

Ingredients:

- 1 (3 to 3½-pound) pork sirloin roast

Directions:

1.   Reduce the size of the pig roast by removing the silver skin and extra fat.

2.   In a sealamble plastic bag or brining container with a gallon capacity, mix the roast and buttermilk brine.

3.   Maintain in the refrigerator for a few days, tossing the roast often.

4.   Remove the pork sirloin roast from the brine and pat it dry using paper towels before cooking.

5. Insert a meat thermometer into the roast's thickest portion.

6. Set your Pit Boss smoker or grill to 225 degrees Fahrenheit and use either apple or cherry Pit Boss to smoke or grill without direct heat.

7. Allow the roast to smoke between 3 and 3 1/2 hours, or until the internal temperature reaches 145 degrees Fahrenheit.

8. Following a 15-minute rest under an uncovered foil tent, cut the roast against the grain.

Cider Brined Grilled Pork Steak

Total Time: 45 minutes

Servings: 2

Recommended pellets: Hickory

Ingredients:

- 4 pork steaks
- 1/3 cup sea salt
- ¼ cup Pit boss AP Rub
- 1 cup maple syrup
- ¼ cup Pit boss BBQ Sauce
- 2 tsp dried thyme
- 1½ cup apple cider
- 1½ cup ice water
- 2 tsp hot sauce
- 1 cup water

Directions:

1. Combine dried thyme, salt, and a third of a cup of maple syrup in a small pot. Maintain a medium heat for about 5 minutes, or until the salt has dissolved and the water has reached a rolling boil.

2. Remove the saucepan from the stove. The ice may be melted by swirling the cider, ice water, and 1 teaspoon of spicy sauce into the ice cubes. Before using brine on the grill, it must be refrigerated to 45 degrees Fahrenheit.

3. Together, seal the bag holding the pork steaks and brine. Refrigerate for at least two hours to enable flavors to blend.4. Combine the remaining maple syrup and spicy sauce with the barbecue sauce in a small dish and set aside. Preheat your Pit boss Grill to 300°F.

4. Using paper towels, blot the pork steaks dry after removing them from the brine. Grill the meat until the first side has nice grill marks, then flip.

5. Internal grill temperature should be between 145 and 160 degrees. Brush the pork steaks using the syrup mixture every 3 minutes throughout the last 10 minutes of cooking.

6. Allow within 5 minutes for the meat to rest before serving.

Smoked Carolina Pulled Pork Sandwiches

Total Time: 8 hours

Portion: 6 - 8

Recommended pellet: hickory

Ingredients:

- 1 bone-in Boston butt (6 - 7 pounds)
- Pork and poultry rub
- 2 cup apple cider vinegar
- 2 cup beer
- 3 tablespoons fresh lemon juice
- 2 tablespoon Worcestershire sauce

- 2 teaspoon red pepper flakes
- Buns

For the sauce and slaw:

- 3 cups apple cider vinegar
- 2 ½ cups water
- ½ cup ketchup
- ¼ cup brown sugar
- 5 teaspoons salt
- 2 - 4 teaspoons red pepper flakes
- 1 teaspoon black pepper (freshly ground)
- 1 teaspoon white pepper (freshly ground)
- ½ cabbage (large, cored, shredded)

Directions:

Grill prep:

1.   Season your pork butt with the rub and make sure the rub gets on every inch.

2.   Wrap up your seasoned butt in plastic and keep in your fridge for 8 hours.

3.   To make your mop sauce, grab a nonreactive bowl and mix your lemon juice, beer, Worcestershire sauce, apple cider vinegar, and red pepper flakes in it. Then set aside.

On the Grill:

1.   Make sure the Smoker grill is set up for indirect heat.

2.   The Smoker grill has to be preheated for 15 minutes at 180 degrees Fahrenheit with the lid closed.

3.   Remove the pork butt from its packaging and place it directly on the grill grate. If you want your meat to taste great, smoke it for three hours and mop it with the mop sauce every hour.

4.   Increasing the head temperature to 250 degrees Fahrenheit, continue roasting the pig until the internal smoke temperature reaches 160 degrees Fahrenheit. Expect another three hours of work. Each hour on the hour, continue scrubbing the floor with the mop sauce.

5.   In order to achieve an internal temperature of 204 degrees Fahrenheit, it is recommended that you cook your pork butt in foil.

6.   If you want to keep your pork warm for up to an hour, you may leave it in the foil it came in, cover it in some thick bath towels, and put it in a cooler.

7.   Apple cider vinegar, ketchup, water, brown sugar, salt, red pepper flakes, white pepper, and black pepper should all be combined in a mixing bowl to form the vinegar sauce. Keep stirring until you no longer see any undissolved salt or sugar crystals.

8.   If it needs extra sugar or red pepper flakes, taste it and adjust the spice accordingly. Then, after an hour, taste how the tastes have blended together.

9.   A typical recipe for Carolina coleslaw calls for 1 cup of the vinegar sauce, 14 cup of diced red onion, and 1 cup each of shredded cabbage and carrots to be mixed together in a dish.

10.   To make pulled pork, first cut the pork into chunks and discard the bone, gristle, and fat. Make pulled pork by shredding the meat and placing it in a disposable roasting pan.

11.   Use the fluids from the foil and part of the vinegar sauce to help the meat stay moist as it cooks.

12.   Put the meat on the buns and the coleslaw on the side. Cook up a storm and feast like kings!

Smoked Pork Burgers

Total Time: 2 hours

Portion: 4

Recommended pellets: hickory

Ingredients:

*   2 lbs. ground pork

*   1/2 of onion finely chopped

*   2 Tbsp. fresh sage, chopped

*   1 tsp. garlic

*   1 tsp. cayenne pepper

*   salt and pepper to taste

Directions:

1.   Start the pellet grill (recommended hickory pellet) on SMOKE with the lid open. Set the temperature to 225 degrees F.

2.   In a bowl, combine ground pork with all remaining ingredients.

3.   Use your hands to mix thoroughly. Form mixture into 8 burgers.

4.   Place the hamburgers on the racks.

5.   Smoked the burgers for 60 to 90 minutes until they reach an internal temperature of 150°F to 160°F (as read by a meat thermometer).

6.   Serve hot.

Smoked Pork Sausages

Total time: 1 hour & 10 minutes

Portion: 6

Recommended Pellet: apple wood

Ingredients:

*   3-pound package of pork mince
*   1/2 tsp. mustard
*   Two garlic cloves, one tablespoon of onion
*   1/2 milligram of red pepper flakes
*   1 tbsp. salt, 1 tbsp. pepper, black
*   1/4 teaspoon of cold water
*   Rinse the pig stomach with cold water in order to soften and drain it.

Direction:

1.   Besides the pig casings, add all other components. Combine the ingredients well.
2.   The meat mixture should be stuffed into the pig casings.
3.   Fill a length of pork casing measuring about 5 inches with the meat mixture. Continue the procedure until sausages are formed.
4.   Prepare the grill by heating the cooktop to 230 degrees Fahrenheit. For 10 minutes, keep the lid covered and the oven warmed.
5.   Smoke the steak on a grill for fifty-five minutes.
6.   Put it in the refrigerator for a time before slicing.

Hot and Tender Pork Sausage Balls

Total Time: 2 hours

Portion: 8

Recommended Pellet: Oak Wood, Alder Wood, Hickory Wood

Ingredients:

*   For the meatballs:

*   Whole milk—½ cup

- Pork sausage—½ lb., mild, ground

- Ground beef—2 ¼ lbs.

- Egg—1

- Chili powder—2 tsps.

- Breadcrumbs—1 cup

- Hot sauce—1 tsp.

- For the sauce:

- Kosher salt

- Olive oil—1 tbsp.

- Water—1 cup

- Ancho chili—1 tsp., powdered

- Yellow onion ½, diced

- Ketchup—2 cups

- Brown sugar—1 ½ cups

- Garlic—1 clove, minced

- Apple cider—3 tbsps.

Directions:

1.   In a large enough mixing bowl, mix the ground sausage, beef, and breadcrumbs.

2.   In a different bowl, prepare a mixture of milk, hot sauce, and egg.

Combine with the sausage mixture and add pepper, salt, and chili powder.

3.   Prepare meatballs and place them on aluminum foil.

4.   Prepare the Smoker grill by preheating it to a Smoke Temperature of about 180°F. Close the top lid and leave for 12–15 minutes.

5.   Put the meatballs in a cast iron pan and transfer to the grilling grate to smoke for about 48–60 minutes.

6.   Heat oil in a large enough saucepan and cook onion with the garlic. Add salt and cook while stirring for about 7–8 minutes. Mix chili powder and keep cooking for another minute or so. Mix brown sugar and simmer slowly to dissolve it completely.

7.   Combine apple cider and ketchup. Simmer this sauce for about 16-20 minutes to achieve the desired consistency.

8.   Remove the pan of smoked meatballs and pour the prepared sauce over them.

9.   Raise the temperature of the smoker-grill to about 300 degrees Fahrenheit.

10.   The meatballs will need 35–45 minutes of cooking time. Remove and top with more sauce before serving.

Chapter 6: LAMB & GAME RECIPES

Seasoned Lamb Shoulder

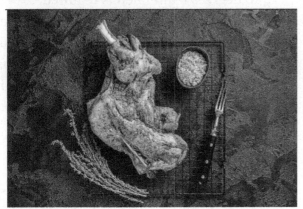

Total Time: 6 hours

Portion: 6

Recommended pellets: Cherry

Ingredients:

• 1 (5-pound) bone-in lamb shoulder, trimmed

• 3-4 tablespoons Moroccan seasoning

• 2 tablespoons olive oil

• 1 cup water

• ¼ cup apple cider vinegar

Directions:

1. For optimal results, preheat your grill to 275 degrees Fahrenheit.
2. Coat the lamb shoulder evenly with oil, then rub it with Moroccan spices.
3. Roast the lamb shoulder under a foil tent for 45 minutes.
4. Shake a bottle of water with some vinegar added to it.
5. The shoulder of lamb will benefit from a spritz of vinegar sauce.
6. Spray the mixture every 20 minutes for four to five hours while cooking.
7. To prepare the lamb shoulder for slicing, remove it off the rack and let it rest for roughly 10 minutes on a cutting board.
8. Shoulder of lamb may be served as slices.

Herby Lamb Chops

Total Time: 2 hours & 10 minutes

Portion: 4

Recommended Pellet: maple

Ingredients:

• 8 lamb chops, each about ¾-inch thick.

For the Marinade:

• 1 teaspoon minced garlic

• Salt to taste

• 1 tablespoon dried rosemary

• Ground black pepper to taste

• ½ tablespoon dried thyme

• 3 tablespoons balsamic vinegar

• 1 tablespoon Dijon mustard

• ½ cup olive oil

Directions:

1.   Prepare the marinade by mixing all of the ingredients carefully.

2.   After putting the lamb chops in a plastic bag, pouring the marinade, and closing the bag, refrigerate for about 4 hours.

3.   After 4 hours have passed, set the grill to smoke and allow it to preheat for about 7 minutes.

4.   The lamb chops should be brought from the refrigerator to room temperature.

5.   When you are ready to cook the ribs, place them on the grill and close the lid so that they may smoke for 5 minutes each side.

6.   After cooking, allow the lamb chops to rest for 5 minutes before serving.

Roasted Leg of Lamb

Total Time: 2 hours & 30 minutes

Portion: 12

Recommended pellets: cherry

Ingredients:

•   8 pounds leg of lamb, bone-in, fat trimmed

•   2 lemons, juiced, with zest

•   1 tablespoon minced garlic

•   4 sprigs of rosemary, 1-inch diced

•   4 cloves of garlic, peeled, sliced lengthwise

•   Salt as needed

•   Ground black pepper as needed

•   2 teaspoons olive oil

Directions:

1.   At least 5 minutes of reheating at 450 degrees Fahrenheit is required.

2.   In the meanwhile, rub the whole leg of lamb with a mixture of minced garlic and oil that has been prepared in a small dish.

3.   Next, cut about two dozen 3/4-inch-deep incisions into the lamb and stuff each with garlic pieces and rosemary. Season with salt and pepper, then sprinkle with lemon zest and drizzle with lemon juice.

4.   The grill should be preheated for 30 minutes before to placing the lamb on the grates to smoke.

5.   Adjust the smoker's temperature to 350 degrees Fahrenheit and smoke for 1 hour and 30 minutes, or until an instant-read thermometer registers 130 degrees Fahrenheit, whichever occurs first.

6.   After cooking, the lamb must rest for 15 minutes before being cut and served.

Crown Rack of Lamb

Total Time: 40 minutes

Portion: 6

Recommended Pellets: hickory

Ingredients:

•   2 racks of lamb, frenched

•   1 tbsp garlic, crushed

•   1 tbsp rosemary, finely chopped

•   1/4 cup olive oil

•   2 feet twine

Directions:

1.   Rinse the racks with cold water then pat them dry with a paper towel.

2.   Lay the racks on a flat board then score between each bone, about ¼ inch down.

3.   In a mixing bowl, mix garlic, rosemary, and oil then generously brush on the lamb.

4.   Take each lamb rack and bend it into a semicircle, forming a crown-like shape.

5.   Use the twine to wrap the racks about 4 times starting from the base to the top. Make sure you tie the twine tightly to keep the racks together.

6.   Preheat the grill to 400-450°F then place the lamb racks on a baking dish.

7.   Grill for 10 minutes then reduce temperature to 300°F. Smoke until the internal temperature reaches 130°F.

8.   Remove the lamb rack from the wood pellet and let rest for 15 minutes.

9.   Serve when hot with veggies and potatoes. Enjoy.

Smoked Pulled Lamb Sliders

Total Time: 9 Hours & 10 minutes

Portion: 7

Recommended pellets: wood pellets

Ingredients:

- 5 lb. lamb shoulder, boneless

- 1/2 cup olive oil

- 1/3 cup kosher salt

- 1/3 cup pepper, coarsely ground

- 1/3 cup granulated garlic

For the spritz

- 4 oz Worcestershire sauce

- 6 oz apple cider vinegar

Directions:

1.   Place a pan of water inside of the Pit Boss and increase the temperature to 225 degrees.

2.   First, any excess fat must be removed from the lamb before it is patted dry using paper towels. Combine oil, salt, pepper, and garlic to make a rub.

3.   Lamb should be smoked in a Pit Boss for 90 minutes, spritzed every 30 minutes, until the internal temperature reaches 165 degrees Fahrenheit.

4.   Place the lamb on a pan made of aluminum foil and pour the remaining spritz liquid over it. Return in foil packaging to the Pit Master.

5.   By smoking, raise the temperature to 250 degrees Fahrenheit.

6.   Before serving, remove the meat from the smoker and place it in a cooler without ice for 30 minutes.

7.   Combine with your preferred slaw and a bread for a delicious supper.

Smoked Lamb Shoulder Chops

Total Time: 4 hours & 30 minutes

Portion: 4

Recommended pellets: Hickory

Ingredients:

- 4 lamb shoulder chops

- 4 cups buttermilk

- 1 cup cold water

- ¼ cup kosher salt

- 2 tablespoons olive oil

- 1 tablespoon Texas style rub

Directions:

1. To produce buttermilk, mix buttermilk, water, and salt in a large bowl until the salt is dissolved.

2. Add chops to the mixture and coat them evenly.

3. Chill in the refrigerator for at least 4 hours. Remove the chops from the plate and submerge them in cold water.

4. Rub olive oil into the ribs, and then sprinkle with seasoning. Set the grill temperature to 240 degrees Fahrenheit.

5. In a pallet grill grate, smoke the chops for 25 to 30 minutes, or until they achieve the desired doneness.

6. Meanwhile, preheat the broiler.

7. Cook the chops under broiler till browned.

Stuffed Leg of Lamb

Total time: 2 hours & 50 minutes

Portion: 8

Recommended Pellet: hickory

Ingredients:

- 1 (8-ounce) carton of softened cream cheese 1/4 cup fried bacon crumbles
- 1 jalapeño pepper, chopped and seeded
- 1 tablespoon of crushed dried rosemary
- Garlic powder, 2 tablespoons of onion powder, 1 teaspoon of paprika, and 1 teaspoon of cayenne pepper.
- A dash of chili pepper
- as required, salt
- 1 butterflied lamb leg (around 4 to 5 pounds)

- Two to Three Tablespoons of Extra Virgin Olive Oil

Directions:

1. Preheat the grill setting to 225-240 degrees F.

2. For the filling: In a bowl, combine all ingredients and mix until well blended.

3. For the spice mixture: in another bowl, mix all ingredients together.

4. Place the leg of lamb onto a smooth surface.

5. Sprinkle the inside of the leg with some spice mixture.

6. Place filling mixture over the inside surface evenly.

7. Roll the leg of lamb tightly, and with butcher's twine, tie the roll to secure the filling.

8. Coat the outer side of the roll with olive oil evenly and then sprinkle with spice mixture.

9. Arrange the leg of lamb on the grate & cook for about 2-2½ hours.

10. Put the leg of the lamb onto a cutting board.

11. With foil, cover the leg of lamb loosely for about 20-25 minutes before serving.

12. Cut the leg of lamb and serve.

Smoked Rabbit

Total Time: 3 hours & 15 minutes

Portion: 5

Recommended Pellets: Alder

Ingredients:

- One cottontail skinned and gutted
- 2 tbsp. salt
- ½ cup white vinegar
- Water as needed

For Rub

- 1 tbsp. garlic powder
- 1 tbsp. cayenne pepper
- 1 tbsp. salt
- One bottle BBQ sauce

Directions:

1. Take a bowl and add kosher salt and white vinegar to make your brine.

2. Pour the brine over your rabbit using a shallow dish and add just enough water to cover the whole rabbit.

3. Let it sit for an hour.

4. Pre-heat your smoker to a temperature of 200 degree.

5. Take a bowl and whisk in the garlic powder, salt, pepper, and cayenne pepper to make the rub.

6. Season the rabbit.

7. Toss your rabbit in your smoker and add the hickory wood to your wood chamber.

8. Let it smoke for two hours and keep adding wood pellets after every 15 minutes.

9. Remove the rabbit from your grill and serve.

Marinated Saddle Of Lamb Fillet

Total Time: 1 hours and 25 minutes

Servings: 3

Recommended pellets: Alder

Ingredients:

- 1 tbsp dried herbs of province
- 1 tsp dried lavender flowers
- ½ tsp black pepper (coarsely ground)
- 3 tbsp olive oil
- 450 g saddle of lamb fillet (4 saddle of lamb fillets)

Direction:

1. Mix the Provence herbs, lavender flowers and pepper with the olive oil in a bowl.

2. Rinse saddle of lamb fillets, pat dry well and place in a shallow bowl. Brush all around with the herb oil and leave to marinate in the refrigerator for at least 1 hour.

3. Grill the fillets for two to three minutes each side, or until cooked through. The next step is to wrap the meat in aluminum foil and wait 5 minutes. Slice in a diagonal fashion and serve.

Lamb Stew

Total Time: 1 hour & 45 minutes

Recommended pellets: Apple

Servings: 4

Ingredients:

- 2 tablespoons olive oil
- 3 lbs. lamb
- 4 cloves garlic
- 1/4 cup tomato paste
- 2 cups beef stock
- 2 tablespoons dried thyme
- 2 bay leaves
- Salt and pepper
- 12 oz. stout beer
- 3 carrots, peeled and diced
- 2 turnip, peeled and chopped
- 1 onions, chopped
- 2 large parsnip, peeled and chopped
- 2 potatoes, chopped

Directions:

1. When ready to cook, set your smoker to 450 deg and preheat.

2. Season your lamb with salt and pepper.

3. Dice the lamb and cook in the smoker in a large pot, eight minutes on each side, before adding garlic, beef stock, thyme, beer, bay leaves, and salt to the mix and cooking for ten minutes.

4. Add the remaining vegetables and cook for another 50 minutes before serving.

Moroccan Kebabs

Total Time: 50 minutes

Servings: 2

Recommended pellets: Mesquite

Ingredients

- 1 cup onions, finely diced
- 1 tablespoon fresh mint, finely diced
- 1/2 teaspoon paprika
- 1/2 teaspoon salt
- 1/2 teaspoon ground coriander
- 1/4 teaspoon ground cinnamon
- Pita Bread
- 2 cloves garlic, minced
- 3 tablespoons cilantro leaves, finely diced
- 1 tablespoon ground cumin
- 1 1/2 lbs. ground lamb

Directions:

1. In a bowl, mix the ingredients except for the pita bread. Mix into meatballs, and skewer each meatball.

2. Next, wet your hands with water and shape the meat into a sausage shape about as large as your thumb. Cover and refrigerate for 30 minutes.

3. When ready to cook, set your smoker grill temperature to 350°F and preheat. Put the kebabs on the smoker and cook for

White Wine Smoked Rabbit Garlic

Total Time: 2 hours & 30 minutes

Portion: 5

Recommended pellets: apple

Ingredients:

- Rabbit (6-lb., 2.7-kg.)

The Marinade

- Olive oil - 1 cup
- Red wine vinegar - 2 tablespoons
- Minced garlic - ¼ cup
- Kosher salt - 2 tablespoons
- Pepper - 1 ½ teaspoon
- Bay leaves - 2
- Fresh rosemary leaves - 2 sprigs
- Lemon juice - 3 tablespoons
- White wine - ¼ cup

Directions:

1. Combine the marinade ingredients-- olive oil, red wine vinegar, minced garlic, kosher salt, pepper, bay leaves, fresh rosemary, lemon juice, and white wine. Mix well.

2. Rub the spice mixture over the rabbit and place it in a disposable aluminum pan.

3. Marinate the rabbit in a plastic bag for at least two hours, ideally overnight. Ensure that the rabbit is refrigerated so that it remains fresh.

4. After 2 hours, take the rabbit out of the refrigerator and thaw it at room temperature.

53

5. Plug the wood pellet smoker and place the wood pellets inside the hopper. Turn the switch on.

6. Set the temperature to 250°F and prepare the wood pellet smoker for indirect heat. Wait until the wood pellet smoker is ready.

7. Insert the aluminum pan with the rabbit into the wood pellet smoker and smoke it for 2 hours.

8. When the internal temperature of the rabbit reaches 165 degrees Fahrenheit (74 degrees Celsius), remove it from the wood pellet smoker and set it on a serving platter.

Smoked Whole Duck

Total Time: 2 hours 45 minutes

Portion: 4

Recommended Pellet: hickory wood

Ingredients:

- 2 tbsp. of baking soda
- 1 tbsp. of Chinese five spices
- 1 thawed duck
- 1 Granny smith cored and diced apple
- 1 quartered sliced orange
- 2 tbsp. of chicken seasoning, divided

Directions:

1. Start by thoroughly washing the duck under cold running water and patting the meat dry with clean paper towels.

2. Combine the Chicken seasoning and the Chinese Five spice then combine with the baking soda for extra crispy skin.

3.   Season the duck from the inside and out.

4.   Tuck the apple and the orange and apple slices into the cavity.

5.   Turn your Wood Pellet Smoker Grill to smoke mode then let the fire catch and set it to about 300°F to preheat.

6.   Place the duck on the grill grate or in a pan. Roast for about 2 ½ hours at a temperature of about 160°F.

7.   Place the foil loosely on top of the duck and let rest for about 15 minutes.

8.   Serve and enjoy your delicious dish!

Smoked Goose Breast Teriyaki

Total Time: 2 hours 30 minutes

Portion: 2

Recommended pellets: cherry

Ingredients

- Goose breast (4-lbs., 1.8-kg.)

The Marinade

- Teriyaki sauce - ½ cup

- Soy sauce - ¼ cup

- Sherry wine - ¼ cup

- Olive oil - 1.2 cup

- Chopped onion - ¼ cup

- Minced garlic - 2 tablespoons

- Ginger powder - 1 teaspoon

- Kosher salt - 1 teaspoon

- Pepper - ½ teaspoon

Directions:

1.   Mix the teriyaki sauce with soy sauce, sherry wine, and olive oil. Stir until incorporated.

2.   Stir into the liquid the chopped onion, minced garlic, ginger powder, kosher salt, and black pepper.

3.   Score the goose breast at several places then put it into the liquid mixture.

4.   Marinate the goose breast for approximately 2 hours and store it in the refrigerator to keep the goose fresh.

5.   After 2 hours, take the goose breast out of the refrigerator and thaw it at room temperature.

6.   Plug the wood pellet smoker and place the wood pellet inside the hopper. Turn the switch on.

7.   Set the temperature to 250°F and prepare the wood pellet smoker for indirect heat. Wait until the wood pellet smoker is ready.

8.   Arrange the marinated goose breast in the wood pellet smoker and smoke it for 2 hours.

9.   Baste the remaining marinade mixture and repeat once every 30 minutes.

10.   When the internal temperature hits 170 degrees Fahrenheit, goose breasts should be removed from the wood pellet smoker (77 degrees Celsius).

Smoked Quails

Total Time: 1 hour 30 minutes

Portion: 4

Recommended Pellets: Alder

Ingredients:

- 5 lbs. quail

FOR MARINADE

- 2 cups orange juice
- 1 cup of soy sauce
- 2 tbsp. garlic, minced
- ½ cup brown sugar
- ¼ cup olive oil
- 1 tbsp. pepper
- 1 cup onion, chopped

Directions:

1. Add orange juice into a container and add soy sauce, garlic, brown sugar, olive oil, pepper, onion, and stir well.

2. Add quail to container and toss well to coat.

3. Cover the container with lid and marinate quail for 3 hours or overnight.

4. Pre-heat your Smoker to 225 degrees F.

5. Add quail (breast side up) and smoke for 1 hour.

6. Once done, remove and serve

7. Enjoy!

Smoked Venison And Boar

Total Time: 5 hours & 5 minutes

Portion: 6

Recommended Pellets: cherry

Ingredients

- 1 lb. of ground wild boar
- 1 lb. of ground venison
- 2 Teaspoons of celery salt
- 2 Teaspoons of red pepper flakes

Directions:

1. Open the smoker's cover and warm it to 225 degrees Fahrenheit for roughly 4 to 5 minutes.

2. Combine all ingredients in a bowl, then form the meat into bars using your hands.

3. Bars must be grilled for about 4 hours.

4. Remove off the grill and put aside for about 5 minutes.

5. Bring out the grub!

Lamb Wraps

Total Time: 3 hours

Portion: 4

Recommended Pellets: Apple

Ingredients:

- 1 leg of lamb
- 3 lemons, juiced
- Olive oil
- Big game rub
- 2 cups yogurt
- 2 cucumbers, diced

- 2 cloves garlic, minced

- 4 tablespoons dill, finely diced

- 2 tablespoons mint leaves, finely diced

- Salt and pepper

- 12 pitas

- 3 tomatoes, diced

- 1 red onion, thinly sliced

- 8 oz. feta cheese

Directions:

1. Rub your lamb with the lemon juice, olive oil, and the rub.

2. When cooking, preheat the smoker to 500 degrees Fahrenheit. Legs of lamb should be smoked for thirty minutes.

3. Continue cooking at 350 degrees Fahrenheit for another hour.

4. While the lamb is roasting, create the tzatziki sauce by mixing the yogurt, cucumbers, garlic, dill, mint leaves in a bowl and mix to combine. Place in the refrigerator to chill.

5. Get the pitas and wrap in foil then place on the grill to warm.

6. Put the lamb on a cutting board and leave to rest for 15 minutes before slicing.

7. Fill the warm pita with red onion, lamb, diced tomato, tzatziki sauce, and feta.

Chapter 7: CHICKEN & POULTRY RECIPES

Maple Glazed Whole Chicken

Total Time: 3 Hours

Portion: 4

Recommended pellets: Cherry or apple

Ingredients:

Ingredients for The Rub:

- Black pepper and salt, to taste
- 3 garlic cloves, minced
- 3 teaspoons of onion powder
- 1.5 teaspoons of ginger, minced
- ½ teaspoon of five-spice powder

Basic Ingredients

- 2.5 pounds whole chicken
- 4 tablespoons of melted butter
- 1 cup of grapefruit juice
- 2.5 cups chicken stock
- Ingredients for The Glaze:
- 6 teaspoons of coconut milk
- 3 tablespoons of sesame oil
- 3 tablespoons of maple syrup
- 1 tablespoon of lemon juice
- 4 tablespoons of melted butter

Directions:

1.   In a small cooking pot, pour the coconut milk and add sesame oil, maple syrup, melted butter, and lemon juice.
2.   Cook the mixture for a few minutes until all the ingredients are combined well. The glaze is ready.
3.   Reserve some of the mixture for further use.
4.   Take a separate cooking pot and add chicken stock, butter, and grapefruit juice.
5.   Simmer the mixture for a few minutes and then add the chicken to this liquid.
6.   Submerge the chicken completely in the brine and let it sit for a few hours for marinating.
7.   In a separate bowl, combine all the rub ingredients.
8.   After a few hours, take out the chicken from the liquid and pat dry with a paper towel.
9.   Now cover the chicken with the rub mixture.
10.   Preheat the smoker grill for 20 minutes at 225 degrees Fahrenheit.
11.   Cherry or apple wood chip can be used to create the smoke.
12.   Place chicken onto the smoker grill grate and cook for 3 hours by closing the lid.
13.   After every 30 minutes, baste the chicken with the maple glaze.
14.   When the internal temperature of chicken reaches 165 degrees Fahrenheit, it is ready to consume.

15.   After removing chicken from the grill, it must be basted with the glaze and more butter.

16.   If you like to serve the chicken at room temperature, allow it to rest for 10 minutes.

Orange Chicken Wings

Total Time: 1 hour and 15 minutes

Portion: 4

Recommended pellets: applewood

Ingredients:

For the Sauce:

- 1 orange, zested

- 1 tablespoon corn starch

- 1 teaspoon ground ginger

- ½ teaspoon salt

- 1/4 teaspoon ground white pepper

- 1/3 cups brown sugar

- 1 tablespoon chili garlic paste

- 2 tablespoons soy sauce

- 1 cup orange juice, fresh

- 1/4 cup chicken stock

For the Wings:

- 2 pounds chicken wings

- 2 tablespoons salt

Directions:

1.   Spread the chicken wings on a wire rack placed on a sheet pan and lined with paper towels, then pat dry the chicken wings, sprinkle with salt and place them in the refrigerator for 1 hour.

2.   When ready to smoke, open the smoker hopper, add the dry pallets, turn on the smoker, and close the ash damper.

3.   Prepare the smoker by preheating it at 300 degrees Fahrenheit for 10 minutes.

4.   The chicken wings should be smoked with the hood closed for 45 minutes, or until the interior temperature reaches 170 degrees Fahrenheit.

5.   In the meanwhile, prepare the orange sauce by combining the chicken stock and corn starch in a bowl. Stir until mixed.

6.   Add remaining ingredients for the sauce in a saucepan, whisk well until combined, then place it over medium heat and bring the sauce to simmer.

7.   Then whisk in corn starch-chicken stock mixture until mixed and continue simmering the sauce for 5 to 10 minutes or until the sauce has thickened; remove the pan from heat and set aside until required.

8.   When chicken wings are done, transfer them to a large bowl, pour in prepared orange sauce, and toss until the chicken wings are well-covered.

9.   Serve straight away.

Chicken Lollipops

Total Time: 2 Hours

Portion: 6

Recommended pellets: Apple

Ingredients:

• 12 chicken lollipops

• Chicken seasoning

• Ten tablespoons butter, sliced into 12 cubes

• 1 cup barbecue sauce

• 1 cup hot sauce

Directions:

1. Turn and Set the grill to 300 degrees F.

3. Then season, the chicken with the chicken seasoning.

4. Arrange the chicken in a baking pan.

5. Put the butter cubes on top of each chicken.

6. Cook the chicken lollipops for 2 hours, basting with the melted butter in the baking pan every 20 minutes.

7. Pour in the barbecue sauce and hot sauce over the chicken.

8. Grill for 15 minutes.

Balsamic Vinegar Chicken Breasts

Total Time: 3 Hours & 10 minutes

Portion: 4

Recommended pellets: applewood

Ingredients:

• 6 tablespoons of olive oil

• 1 cup balsamic vinegar

• 3 cloves of garlic cloves, minced

• 1 teaspoon of basil, fresh

• 1 teaspoon of chili powder

• Salt and black pepper, to taste

• 2 pounds of chicken breast, boneless and skinless

Directions:

1. In a zip lock bag, add oil, balsamic vinegar, basil leaves, chili powder, garlic cloves, salt, and black pepper.

2. Now, place the chicken in the zip lock bag and mix well.

3. Marinate the chicken in the sauce for 3 hours in the refrigerator.

4. Now, preheat the grill for 20 minutes at 225 degrees F.

5. Place the chicken onto the grill and smoke for 3 hours.

6. once the 3 hours have passed take it off the grill and serve. Enjoy

Smoked Chicken in Maple Flavor

Total Time: 6 Hours

Portion: 3

Recommended pellets: maple

Ingredients:

• Boneless chicken breast (5-lbs., 2.3-kgs)

• The Spice

• 1 tablespoon Chipotle powder

- Salt – 1 ½ teaspoons
- 2 teaspoons Garlic powder
- 2 teaspoons Onion powder
- Pepper – 1 teaspoon
- The Glaze
- Maple syrup – ½ cup
- The Fire
- Preheat the smoker an hour prior to smoking.
- Use charcoal and maple wood chips for smoking.

Directions:

1.   Preheat a smoker to 225°F (107°C) with charcoal and maple wood chips.

2.   Place chipotle, salt, garlic powder, onion powder, and pepper in a bowl then mix to combine.

3.   Rub the chicken with the spice mixture then place on the smoker's rack.

4.   Smoke the chicken for 4 hours and brush with maple syrup once every hour.

5.   When the internal temperature has reached 170°F , remove the smoked chicken breast from the smoker and transfer to a serving dish.

6.   Serve and enjoy right away.

Lemon Chicken

Total Time: 19 minutes

Servings: 6

Recommended pellets: Pecan

Ingredients:

- 2 teaspoons honey

- 1 tablespoon lemon juice
- 1 teaspoon lemon zest
- 1 clove garlic, coarsely chopped
- 2 sprigs thyme
- Salt and pepper to taste
- ½ cup olive oil
- 6 chicken breast fillets

Directions:

1.   Combine honey, lemon juice and zest, garlic, thyme, salt, and pepper to create a sauce.

2.   Olive oil should be added gradually to the mixture.

3.   The liquid should be used to marinade chicken fillets.

4.   Cover and refrigerate for 4 hours.

5.   With the hood closed, warm the smoker to 400 degrees Fahrenheit for 10 minutes.

6.   Each side of the chicken should be cooked for 5 minutes.

7.   Make additional marinade to use as a basting sauce when cooking.

Bacon-Wrapped Chicken Tenders

Total Time: 45 minutes

Servings: 6

Recommended pellets: Hickory

Ingredients:

- Breasts of chicken weighing 1 pound
- About 10 slices of bacon
- Ingredients: 1/2 teaspoon Italian Black pepper sprinkling equal to one-half teaspoon

- 1.75 tablespoons of salt Two spoonfuls of paprika
- 1 tablespoon onion powder
- 1 teaspoon Garlic Powder
- Approximately one-fifth of a cup of mild brown sugar
- 1 tablespoon chili powder

Directions:

1. Preheat your smoker to 350°F.

2. Mix seasonings

3. Sprinkle the mixture on all sides of chicken tenders

4. Wrap each chicken tender with a strip of bacon

5. Mix sugar and chili then sprinkle the mixture on the bacon-wrapped chicken.

6. Place them on the smoker and smoker for 30 minutes with the lid closed or until the chicken is cooked.

7. Serve and enjoy.

Hot and Spicy Smoked Chicken Wings

Total Time: 3 Hours

Portion: 5

Recommended pellets: hickory

Ingredients:

- Chicken wings (6-lbs., 2.7-kgs)
- The Rub
- Olive oil – 3 tablespoons
- Chili powder – 2 ½ tablespoons
- Smoked paprika – 3 tablespoons
- Cumin – ½ teaspoon
- Garlic powder – 2 teaspoons
- Salt – 1 ¾ teaspoons
- Pepper – 1 tablespoon
- Cayenne – 2 teaspoons
- The Fire
- Preheat the smoker an hour prior to smoking.
- Add soaked hickory wood chips during the smoking time.

Directions:

1. Separate and place the chicken wings in separate dishes. For the time being, disregard.

2. Add chili powder, smoked paprika, cumin, garlic powder, salt, pepper, and cayenne pepper to olive oil and mix completely.

3. After applying the rub, the chicken wings should rest in the spice mixture for at least one hour for optimal results.

4. Utilize charcoal and hickory wood chips to smoke the meat at 225 degrees Fahrenheit (107 degrees Celsius) Start the indirect heat.

5. When ready, lay the chicken wings on the rack of the smoker.

6. Smoke the wings for two hours, or until an instant-read thermometer reveals an internal temperature of 160 degrees Fahrenheit (71 degrees Celsius).

7. Remove the wings from the smoker and set them on a serving plate before serving.

8. Serve immediately and taste.

Spiced Lemon Chicken

Total Time: 5 Hours

Portion: 4

Recommended pellets: hickory

Ingredients:

- 1 chicken, uncut
- 4 minced cloves of garlic
- A sprinkle of salt and the rinds of two lemons are added to a dish.
- Extra-virgin olive oil, 1 tablespoon
- A teaspoon of smoked paprika
- a quarter teaspoon of salt
- 1/2 teaspoon ground black pepper
- 12 teaspoons of oregano
- One Tablespoon of Ground Cumin

Directions:

1. Preheat the grill by pushing the temperature to 375 degrees F.

2. Now take the chicken and spatchcock it by cutting it on both sides from the backbone to the tail via the neck.

3. Lay it flat and push it down on the breastbone. This would break the ribs.

4. Place all the leftover ingredients in a bowl, except ½ teaspoon of salt, and crush them to make a smooth rub.

5. Spread this rub evenly over the chicken, making sure that it seeps right under the skin.

6. Now put the chicken on the grill and let it smoke for one hour.

7. Let it stand for 5 minutes.

8. Serve and enjoy.

Hickory Spatchcock Turkey

Total Time: 3-4 hours

Portion: 8-10

Recommended pellets: Hickory

Ingredients:

- 1 (14 lb.) fresh or thawed frozen young turkey

- 1/4 cup flavored extra virgin olive oil with roasted garlic

- 6 poultry seasonings or original dry lab in January

Directions:

1. Grill at 250 degrees for 5 minutes.
2. The turkey skin should be placed on a fiberglass grill mat coated with Teflon.
3. The turkey must be roasted at 225 degrees Fahrenheit for two hours.
4. After one hour, the temperature of the pit should be raised to 350 degrees Fahrenheit.
5. The turkey should be cooked until an instant-read thermometer inserted into the thickest region of the breast registers 165 degrees Fahrenheit and the juices flow clear.
6. Before cutting the Hickory-smoked turkey, tent it gently with aluminum foil for 20 minutes.

Slow Roasted Shawarma

Total Time: 4 Hours

Portion: 3

Recommended pellets: hickory

Ingredients:

- 5 ½ lbs. of chicken thighs; boneless, skinless

- 4 ½ lbs. of lamb fat

- Pita bread

- 5 ½ lbs. of top sirloin

- 2 yellow onions; large

- 4 tablespoons of rub

- Desired toppings like pickles, tomatoes, fries, salad and more

Directions:

1.   Slice the meat and fat into ½ inch slices and place them in 3 separate bowls

2.   Season each of the bowls with the rub and massage the rub into the meat to make sure it seeps well.

3.   Now place half of the onion at the base of each half skewer. This will make for a firm base.

4.   Add 2 layers from each of the bowls at a time.

5.   Make the track as symmetrical as you can.

6.   Now, put the other 2 half onions at the top of this.

7.   After wrapping in plastic, refrigerate overnight.

8.   Start preheating the grill to 275 degrees Fahrenheit.

9.   The shawarma must grill for about 4 hours after being placed on the grill. Perform at least one complete spin.

10.   Remove the meat off the grill and increase the heat to 445 degrees.

11.   Now, heat some olive oil on a griddle made of cast iron and place it on the grill.

12.   When the griddle has turned hot, place the whole shawarma on the cast iron and smoke it for 5 to 10 minutes per side.

13.   Remove from the grill and slice off the edges.

14.   Repeat the same with the leftover shawarma.

15.   Serve in pita bread and add chosen toppings.

16.   Enjoy.

Grilled Chicken Kebabs

Total Time: 40 minutes

Portion: 8

Recommended pellets: hickory

Ingredients:

For Marinade

- Olive oil - ½ cup
- One tablespoon of lemon juice.
- 1.5 tablespoons of vinegar
- Seasoning salt: 1 1/2 teaspoons
- two teaspoons of garlic mince
- About 1.5 milligrams of fresh thyme
- Two teaspoons' worth of fresh Italian parsley
- 1 teaspoon chopped dry chili pepper
- 2 teaspoons fresh chopped chives
- Ground pepper - ½ tablespoon

For Kebabs

- Orange, yellow, and red bell peppers
- Chicken breasts - 1 ½, boneless and skinless
- Mushrooms of your choice - 10-12 medium size

Directions:

1.   To prepare the marinade, mix all the ingredients together.

2.   Place the marinade in the refrigerator before combining the chicken and mushrooms.

3.   Raise the temperature on your wood pellet grill to 450 degrees.

4.   Once the chicken has been marinated, remove it from the refrigerator and place it on the grill.

5.   Grill the kebabs for 6 minutes on one side. To cook the other side of the meat, flip it over.

6.   Enjoy with your choice of accompaniment.

Smoked Queso Dip with Pulled Chicken

Cooking Time: 65 Minutes

Recommended pellets: Apple

Portion: 6

Ingredients:

●   To taste, ale house beer can chicken seasoning

●   1 lb. chicken breasts, boneless, skinless

●   1 tablespoon cilantro, chopped

●   1 tsp cumin, ground

●   2 jalapeños, chopped

●   2 tsp olive oil

●   1 bag tortilla chips

●   1 lb. white American cheese, cubed

●   1 cup milk

Directions:

1.   Turn on SMOKE mode and let the Pit Boss pellet grill heat to 350 degrees Fahrenheit with the lid open for 10 minutes. If using a charcoal or gas grill, preheat it to medium heat.

2.   Season the chicken with Ale House Beer Can Chicken after scoring it and rubbing it with olive oil.

3.   Cook the chicken for 8 to 10 minutes on the grill, rotating once or twice.

4.   Reduce the grill temperature to 225° F after removing the chicken from the grill. Before being ripped apart with forks, chicken must rest for 10 minutes.

5.   While the chicken is resting, heat a cast-iron pan on the grill.. Partially open the sear slide, then add the cubed cheese, jalapeno, milk, and cumin to the skillet. 5 minutes, stirring periodically until the cheese melts. Smoker the dip for 40 minutes after folding in the pulled chicken.

6.   Remove from heat and set aside to thicken for 5-10 minutes. Serve with tortilla chips and fresh cilantro on the side.

Smoked Chicken Burgers

Total Time: 1 hour and 10 minutes

Portion: 6

Recommended pellets: oak or apple pellets

Ingredients:

●   2 lb. ground chicken breast

●   2/3 cup of finely chopped onions

●   1 tbsp. of cilantro, finely chopped

●   2 tbsps. fresh parsley, finely chopped

●   2 tbsps. of olive oil

●   1/2 tsp. of ground cumin

●   2 tbsps. of lemon juice freshly squeezed

- 3/4 tsp. of salt and red pepper to taste

Directions:

1. In a bowl, add all ingredients; mix until combined well.

2. Form the mixture into 6 patties.

3. Start your pellet grill on SMOKE (oak or apple pellets). Set the heat to 350°F and preheat.

4. Smoke the chicken burgers for 45-50 minutes or until cooked through, turning every 15 minutes.

5. Your burgers are ready when the internal temperature (as read by a meat thermometer) reaches 165°F.

6. Serve hot.

Herbed Turkey Breast

Total Time: 11 hours

Portion: 12

Recommended pellets: alder

Ingredients:

- 7 pounds turkey breast, bone-in, skin-on, fat trimmed

- 3/4 ounce of sugar

- Approximately one-third of a cup of brown sugar

- Add 4 quarts of cold water.

To make Herb Butter:

- One teaspoon of fresh parsley, half a teaspoon of ground black pepper, chopped

- 8 tablespoons butter, unsalted, softened

- 1 tablespoon chopped sage

- ½ tablespoon minced garlic

- 1 tablespoon chopped rosemary

- 1 teaspoon lemon zest

- 1 tablespoon chopped oregano

- 1 tablespoon lemon juice

Directions:

1. Combine water, salt, and sugar in a large container and mix until the salt and sugar are dissolved to make brine.

2. Place turkey breasts in brine, cover, and chill for a minimum of 8 hours.

3. The next step is to remove the turkey breast from the brine and pat it dry.

4. Open smoker hopper, dry pallets put, ash can in place, open ash damper, smoker started on, open ash damper.

5. Adjust the smoker's temperature to 345 degrees and let it to heat for 28 minutes, or until the green light illuminates.

6. In the meanwhile, place the turkey breast on a metal rack in a roasting pan with 1 cup of water.

7. Prepare the herb butter by putting the butter in a heat-safe container and adding the other ingredients.

8. Loosen the skin at the sternum of the turkey breast with your fingertips. Then, evenly sprinkle three tablespoons of the herb butter, being careful to eliminate any air pockets.

9. Melt the remaining herb butter in the bowl by heating it over high heat for two minutes.

10. The turkey breast is smoked by coating it with melted herb butter and putting it on a smoker pan.

11.   Smoke the turkey for 2 hours and 40 minutes, turning it and basting it every 1 hour and 30 minutes with melted herb butter. This should brown the turkey breast thoroughly.

12.   Transfer the cooked meat to a cutting board, cover, and rest for 15 minutes before slicing and serving.

Bone In-Turkey Breast

Total Time: 3-4 hours

Portion: 6-8

Recommended pellets: Hickory, Mesquite, Applewood, Oak

Ingredients:

- 1 (8-10 pounds) boned turkey breast
- 6 tablespoons extra virgin olive oil
- 5 Yang original dry lab or poultry seasonings

Directions:

1.   As you set up indirect heat on your wood pellet smoker grill, heat some hickory or pecan pellets to 230 degrees Fahrenheit.

2.   Smoke the boned turkey breast directly in a V rack or grill at 225 ° F for 2 hours.

3.   After 2 hours of hickory smoke, raise the pit temperature to 325 ° F. Roast until the thickest part of the turkey breast reaches an internal temperature of 165° F, and the juices are clear.

4.   Place the hickory smoked turkey breast under a loose foil tent for 20 minutes then scrape the grain.

Buffalo Wings

Total Time: 1 hour

Portion: 8

Recommended pellets: Hickory

Ingredients:

Ingredient for Chicken Wings:

- 4 pounds of Chicken Wings
- 2 teaspoons of Corn Starch
- 2 tablespoons of buffalo wings rub
- Salt, To Taste

Ingredients for Buffalo Sauce:

- 1/3 cup Spicy Mustard
- 1 Cup Franks Red Hot Sauce
- 8 tablespoons of Unsalted Butter

Side:

- 1 cup Blue cheese dressing

Directions:

1.   Preheat the grill to 375 degrees F for 15 minutes.

2.   Meanwhile, add wings to a large bowl and sprinkle corn starch, spice rub, and salt.

3.   Mix the ingredients well.

4.   Smoke the wings for 38 minutes after placing them on the grill grate.

5.   Meanwhile, in a bowl, mix all the buffalo sauce ingredients.

6.   Put the sauce over the wings and then cook the wings for an additional 15 minutes with the lid closed.

7.   Serve the wings with blue cheese dressing.

8.   Enjoy.

Chapter 8: FISH & SEAFOOD RECIPES

Garlic Dill Smoked Salmon

Total Time: 4 hours

Portion: 12

Recommended pellets: Rawhide Junior Wood Pellets, Crescent Cooking Hardwood Pellets, Maple Wood Pellet

Ingredients:

- 2 salmon fillets
- Brine
- 4 fluid ounces of water
- 1 ounce of brown sugar
- 1/3 teaspoon of table salt
- Seasoning
- 3 tbsp minced garlic
- 1 tbsp fresh dill, chopped

Directions:

1.   In a plastic bag, combine all brine ingredients until the sugar is dissolved. Seal the bag and refrigerate the salmon overnight.

2.   Remove the fish from the brine and pat it dry. In two to four hours at room temperature, it will be ready for consumption.

3.   Season the salmon with garlic and dill generously.

4.   Fire up the smoker and place the salmon on a cooling rack that is coated with cooking spray.

5.   Place the rack in the smoker and close the lid.

6.   Smoke the salmon for 4 hours until the smoke is 130-180°F.

7.   Remove the salmon and serve with crackers. Enjoy.

Smoked Trout

Total Time: 2 hours

Portion: 4

Recommended pellets: hickory

Ingredients:

6 to 8 rainbow trout

1-gallon water

¼ cup of dark brown sugar

2 tablespoon ground black pepper

3 tablespoons soy sauce

Directions:

1.   Make some butterfly incisions in the fish that has been cleaned.

2.   To prepare the brine, mix the water, brown sugar, soy sauce, and salt and pepper together in a mixing bowl. After brining the fish for one hour, it should be stored in the refrigerator.

3.   15 minutes on the grill at a temperature of 225 degrees Fahrenheit with the lid covered.

4.   The fish has to be washed and patted dry before being served.

5.   Fish may be cooked on the grill in as little as an hour and a half or as much as

two hours, depending on the thickness of the trout.

6.   When the fish becomes opaque and starts to flake, it is ready to be eaten. You may serve it either warm or cold, whatever you want. Enjoy!

Grilled Salmon Fillet

Total Time: 15 minutes

Portion: 4

Recommended pellets: hickory, cherry or oak

Ingredients:

- 1 ½ lb. of salmon fillets
- 4/5 teaspoon salt
- 2/4 teaspoon pepper
- 1 tablespoons butter

Directions:

1.   After skinning the fish, season both sides liberally with salt and pepper. If the chicken is unpeeled, season with salt and pepper. Spread the melted butter on all sides of the fish (olive oil may be used).

2.   Place the fish on the grill at 400-450°F (204-232°C), skin side down (it will not matter which side, if it's skinless).

3.   After 8 minutes (for a 1-inch filet), turn the fish over. Peel the outer layer to remove it. Consider turning the fish over for a few minutes before trying to remove it again if it proves tough to remove. After removing the skin, lightly season with salt and pepper. Use butter for basting. Keep it in the oven for a further 5-6 minutes, then turn it and cook for an additional 2 minutes. Indicate doneness by testing the center with a fork to check whether it separates readily to determine doneness.

The center of the fish should be slightly pink and contain very little liquid. It will continue to cook for up to 5 minutes after being removed from the grill; thus, cover it and allow it to stand uncovered.

4.   Remember that salmon, like all fish, cooks quickly. Make sure you are ready when you start to grill. I always make sure to have my aluminum foil out and ready and any supplies I might need while grilling. You do not want to be stranded looking for tongs while your fish overcooks in the meantime. Be prepared for quick cook time and all will turn out well. Perfect!

Juicy Lime Smoked Tuna Belly

Total Time: 2 hours & 10 minutes

Portion: 10

Recommended pellets: hickory

Ingredients:

- Tuna belly (3-lb., 1.4-kg.)

The Marinade:

- 2 fresh limes
- 2 tablespoons white sugar
- 3 tablespoons brown sugar
- ½ teaspoon pepper
- 1 tablespoon soy sauce
- 2 tablespoons sriracha sauce

Directions:

1.   Cut the limes into halves then squeeze the juice over the tuna belly. Marinate the tuna belly with the juice for 10 minutes. Meanwhile, combine white sugar with brown sugar, pepper, soy sauce, and sriracha sauce, then mix well. Wash and

rinse the tuna belly then pat it dry. Plug the wood pellet smoker then fill the hopper with the wood pellet. Turn the switch on.

2. Set the wood pellet smoker for indirect heat then adjust the temperature to 225°F (107°C).

3. Wait until the wood pellet smoker reaches the desired temperature then place the seasoned tuna belly in it. Smoke the tuna belly for 2 hours or until it flakes, and once it is done, remove it from the wood pellet smoker.

4. Serve and enjoy.

Grilled Fresh Fish

Total Time: 12 to 15 minutes

Portion: 2

Recommended pellets: Hickory or Mesquite

Ingredients:

- 1 cup soy sauce
- 1/3 cup extra-virgin olive oil
- 1 tablespoon minced garlic
- Juice of 2 medium lemons
- 1 stalk fresh basil
- 4 pounds (1.8 kg) fresh fish, cut into portion-sized pieces

Direction:

1. Cover the grill for 15 minutes while preheating it to 225 degrees Fahrenheit.
2. In a large dish, add everything except the fish and stir well. The fish should be marinated for forty minutes.
3. After removing the fish from the marinade, grill it.

4. After 12 to 15 minutes on the grill, the meat should achieve an internal temperature of 140 degrees Fahrenheit (60 degrees Celsius).
5. Designed for immediate consumption.

Swordfish Steaks with Corn Salsa

Total Time: 30 to 33 minutes

Portion: 4

Recommended pellets: Alder

Ingredients:

- 4 whole ears corn, husked
- Olive oil to taste
- Salt and black pepper, to taste
- 1/2 pint cherry tomatoes
- 2 serrano chile, chopped
- 1 red onion, diced
- 1/2 lime, juiced
- 4 swordfish fillets

Direction:

1. Keeping the grill's lid closed, preheat it to 225 degrees Fahrenheit for 10 minutes.
2. Season the corn cobs with salt and pepper before applying olive oil. Prepare the grill and cook the corn for twelve to fifteen minutes.
3. After the corn has cooled, remove the kernels and set them in a medium dish. Incorporate lime juice, red onion, tomatoes, and serrano peppers.
4. In a large bowl, combine the olive oil, salt, and pepper. The mixture is applied to the swordfish fillets.

5.   Simply place the fillets on the grill and allow them to cook for 18 minutes.

6.   Serve the swordfish above the grill after tossing it with the corn salsa.

Grilled King Crab Legs

Total Time: 25 minutes

Portion: 4

Recommended pellets: Oak , Alder Wood Pellets, Mesquite

Ingredients:

- 4 pounds king crab legs (split)
- 3 tbsp lemon juice
- 2 1/2 tbsp garlic powder
- 1 cup butter (melted)
- 2 tsp brown sugar
- 2 tsp paprika
- Black pepper

Directions:

1.   Mix the lemon juice, butter, sugar, garlic, paprika, and pepper together in a bowl.

2.   Arrange the split crab on a baking sheet, split side up. Drizzle ¾ of the butter mixture over the crab legs. Preheat it to 250°F.

3.   Arrange the crab legs onto the grill grate, shell side down. Cover the grill and cook 25 minutes.

4.   Remove the crab legs from the grill. Serve and top with the remaining butter mixture.

Cajun Smoked Shrimp

Total Time: 10 minutes

Portion: 2

Recommended pellets: cherry, hickory

Ingredients:

- 2 tablespoons of virgin olive oil
- 1/2 lemon, juiced
- 3 cloves garlic, finely minced
- 2 tablespoons of Cajun spice
- Salt, to taste
- 1.5 pounds of shrimp, raw, peeled, deveined

Directions:

1.   Take a Ziploc bag and combine olive oil, lemon juice, garlic cloves, Cajun spice, salt, and shrimps.

2.   Toss the ingredients well for fine coating.

3.   Preheat the smoker grill for 10 minutes until the smoke starts to establish.

4.   Just throw the fish on the grill and cover it.

5.   Turn the temperature to high and allow the fish to cook the shrimp for 10 minutes, 5 minutes per side.

6.   Once done, serve.

Teriyaki Smoked Shrimp

Total Time: 10 minutes

Portion: 6

Recommended pellets: Hickory or Pecan

Ingredients:

- 1 lb. tail-on shrimp, uncooked
- 1/2 tbsp onion powder
- 1/2 tbsp salt
- 1/2 tbsp Garlic powder
- 4 tbsp Teriyaki sauce
- 4 tbsp sriracha mayo
- 2 tbsp green onion, minced

Directions:

1. Peel the shrimps leaving the tails then wash them removing any vein. Drain and pat with a paper towel to drain.

2. Preheat the grill to 450°F.

3. Season the shrimp with onion, salt, and garlic then place it on the grill to cook for 5 minute.

4. Take shrimp off grill and stir-fry with teriyaki sauce. Serve garnished with mayo and onions. Enjoy.

Bbq Oysters

Total Time: 16 minutes

Portion: 4-6

Recommended pellets: Hickory, Mesquite

Ingredients:

- Shucked oysters - 12
- Unsalted butter - 1 lb.
- Chopped green onions - 1 bunch
- Honey Hog BBQ Rub or Meat Church "The Gospel" - 1 tbsp
- Minced green onions - ½ bunch
- Seasoned breadcrumbs - ½ cup
- Cloves of minced garlic - 2
- Shredded pepper jack cheese - 8 oz
- Heat and Sweet BBQ sauce

Directions:

1. Preheat the smoker for about 10-15 minutes with the lid closed.

2. To make the compound butter, wait for the butter to soften. Then combine the butter, onions, BBQ rub, and garlic thoroughly.

3. Lay the butter evenly on plastic wrap or parchment paper. Roll it up in a log shape and tie the ends with butcher's twine. Place these in the freezer to solidify for an hour. This butter can be used on any kind of grilled meat to enhance its flavor. Any other high-quality butter can also replace this compound butter.

4.   Shuck the oysters, keeping the juice in the shell.

5.   Sprinkle all the oysters with breadcrumbs and place them directly on the grill. Allow them to cook for 5 minutes. You will know they are cooked when the oysters begin to curl slightly at the edges.

6.   Once they are cooked, put a spoonful of the compound butter on the oysters. Once the butter melts, you can add a little bit of pepper jack cheese to add more flavor to them.

7.   The oysters must not be on the grill for longer than 6 minutes, or you risk overcooking them. Put a generous squirt of the BBQ sauce on all the oysters. Also, add a few chopped onions.

8.   Allow them to cool for a few minutes and enjoy the taste of the sea!

Chapter 9: VEGETABLES

Grilled Corn with Honey and Butter

Total Time: 8 Minutes

Portion: 4

Recommended pellets: Alder Wood Pellets

Ingredients:

- Six pieces of corn
- Two tablespoons olive oil
- 1/2 cup butter
- 1/2 cup honey
- One tablespoon smoked salt
- Pepper to taste

Directions:

1.   Ten to fifteen minutes with the lid closed will get the smoker nice and hot.

2.   Brush the corn with oil and butter.

3.   Grill the corn for 10 minutes, turning from time to time.

4.   Mix honey and butter.

5.   Brush corn with this mixture and sprinkle with smoked salt and pepper.

Cauliflower With Parmesan And Butter

Total Time: 45 Minutes

Portion: 4

Recommended pellets: hardwood, oak or hickory

Ingredients:

•   One medium-sized cauliflower head One teaspoon of garlic powder
•   One-half teaspoon of pepper and one grain of salt
•   a quarter cup of olive oil
•   Unsalted butter (one-half cup).
•   1/4 cup of grated Parmesan cheese and parsley that has been melted.

Directions:

1.   Close the lid and let the smoker to preheat for at least 10 minutes, ideally 15 minutes.
2.   To prepare cauliflower, spray oil over it and season with salt and pepper.
3.   When the grill reaches the correct temperature, remove the cover and place the pan on it. Simply place the vegetables inside, cover, and let them rest for 45 minutes to smoke them.
4.   In the meanwhile, melt the butter in a bowl and stir in the garlic, parsley, and cheese until well-combined.
5.   In the last 20 minutes of cooking, baste the cauliflower regularly with the cheese mixture; then, remove the pan from the heat and garnish with parsley.
6.   It was sliced and placed on the table.

Smoked Vegetables

Total Time: 15 Minutes

Portion: 6

Recommended pellets: pecan

Ingredients:

- 1 fresh ear of corn, stripped of husk and silken strands

- 1 yellow squash

- 2 red onion

- 2 green bell bell pepper

- 2 red bell bell pepper

- 1 yellow bell bell pepper

- 1 cup mushrooms

- 2 tablespoons oil

- 2 tablespoons chicken seasoning

Directions:

1.   Heat the grill until smoke begins to escape from the wood chips.

2.   Sauté the vegetables with the oil and seasonings, then transfer them to the grill.

3.   Cook the meat for 10 minutes, turning the meat occasionally. Cook and enjoy your dinner.

Twice-Smoked Potatoes

Total Time: 14 Minutes

Portion: 4

Recommended pellets: hickory, pecan

Ingredients:

- 8 Idaho, Russet, or Yukon Gold potatoes

- 1 (12-ounce) can evaporate milk, heated
- 1 cup (2 sticks) butter, melted
- ½ cup sour cream, at room temperature
- 1 cup grated Parmesan cheese
- ½ pound bacon, cooked and crumbled
- ¼ cup chopped scallions
- Salt
- Freshly ground black pepper
- 1 cup shredded Cheddar cheese

Directions:

1.   Close the cover and heat the container to 400 degrees Fahrenheit.

2.   Apply vigorous probing with a fork to the potatoes. Place them in a single layer on a covered grill and cook for 1 hour and 15 minutes.

3.   After the potatoes have cooled for 10 minutes, cut them in half along their length.

4.   Place the potato flesh in a bowl and remove the potato skins, leaving about a quarter-inch. Prepare a baking sheet by lining it with the shells.

5.   Add Parmesan cheese, bacon, and scallions after seasoning with salt and pepper.

6.   Evenly distribute the potato mixture and melted Cheddar cheese among the shells.

7.   To grill, place the covered pan on top of the grill for twenty minutes.

Smoked And Smashed Potatoes

Total Time: 8 hours

Portion: 4

Recommended pellets: Mighty Oak

Ingredients:

- 1-1/2 pounds small new red potatoes or fingerlings
- Extra virgin olive oil
- Sea salt and black pepper
- 2 tbsp softened butter

Directions:

1. Let the potatoes dry. Once dried, put in a pan and coat with salt, pepper, and extra virgin olive oil.

2. Place the potatoes on the topmost rack of the smoker.

3. Smoke for 60 minutes.

4. Once done, take them out and smash each one.

5. Mix with butter and season.

Roasted Tomatoes with Hot Pepper Sauce

Total Time: 90 minutes

Portion: 4-6

Recommended pellets: pecan

Ingredients:

- 2 lbs. roman fresh tomatoes
- 3 tbsp. parsley, chopped
- 2 tbsp. garlic, chopped
- Black pepper, to taste
- 1/2 cup olive oil
- Hot pepper, to taste
- 1 lb. spaghetti or other pasta

Directions:

1. Before cooking, preheat the grill with the cover closed for 15 minutes.

2. Wash tomatoes and slice them in half, lengthwise. Put them in a baking dish cut side up.

3. Sprinkle with chopped parsley, garlic, add salt and black pepper, and pour 1/4 cup of olive oil over them.

4. Place on pre-heated Wood Pellet Grill and bake for 1 1/2 hours.

5. Take tomatoes from baking dish and place in a food processor, leaving the cooked oil, and puree them.

6. Drop pasta into boiling salted water and cook until tender. Drain and toss immediately with the pureed tomatoes.

7. Add the remaining 1/4 cup of raw olive oil and crumbled hot red pepper to taste. Toss and serve. Enjoy!

Smoked Mushrooms

Total Time: 45 minutes

Portion: 5

Recommended pellets: hickory

Ingredients:

4 cups of Portobello

1 tablespoon canola oil

1 tablespoon onion

1 tablespoon garlic

1 tablespoon salt

1 tablespoon pepper

Directions:

1.   Put all ingredients in a bowl and mix to incorporate.

2.   Set the grill temperature to 175 degrees Fahrenheit and then add the mushrooms.

3.   Prepare to spend twenty-five minutes smoking these.

4.   After 18 minutes, increase the temperature to 180 degrees and continue cooking.

5.   Cook and enjoy your dinner.

Grilled Zucchini Squash Spears

Total Time: 10 minutes.

Portion: 5

Recommended pellets: apple

Ingredients:

- 4 zucchini, cleaned and cut off at the ends

- 2 tablespoons olive oil

- 2 tablespoon sherry vinegar

- 3 pulled thyme leaves

- Salt and pepper

Directions:

1.   Cut zucchini lengthwise in half and then into thin slices.

2.   Place the zucchini pieces and the other ingredients in a plastic bag. Mix well by tossing.

3.   Turn the wood pellet burner on high and let it to heat up to 350 degrees Fahrenheit for 15 minutes with the lid closed.

4.   Take the zucchini out of the bag and place it on the grill, cut side down.

5.   After 4 minutes, the zucchini will be ready.

6.   Remove the food off the grill and sprinkle it with thyme leaves. Enjoy.

Chapter 10: APPETIZERS

Smoked Olives

Total Time: 2 hours

Recommended pellets: Hickory

Serving: 6

Ingredients:

- 2 cup green olives
- 2 tablespoons oil
- 2 tablespoons white wine
- 2 minced garlic cloves
- ¾ tablespoons dried rosemary
- ¼ tablespoons red pepper flakes

Direction:

1. Preheat your wood pellet grill to 220 degrees Fahrenheit.
2. Combine the ingredients on a tray made of durable aluminum foil.
3. The olives are grilled for two hours.
4. Cook and enjoy your dinner.

Regardless matter the kind of cheese chosen, grilled olives would go nicely with it.

Hint for Variation: Include more Preferred Herbs.

Smoked Herb Popcorn

Total Time: 15 minutes

Serving: 2

Recommended pellets: Cherry

Ingredients:

- 4 tbsp butter
- 2 tsp Italian seasoning, finely crumbled
- 1 tsp garlic powder
- 1 tsp salt
- ¼ cup popcorn kernels
- ½ cup Parmesan cheese, grated

Direction:

1. When you are ready to cook, give the Pit boss a warmup of fifteen minutes with the lid closed at a temperature of two hundred fifty degrees Fahrenheit.
2. Utilize a small pot that is put over medium heat in order to melt the butter. Be sure to thoroughly combine the salt, garlic powder, and Italian seasoning. Take the skillet off the burner and set it somewhere else.
3. Put one-quarter cup of popcorn in a brown paper bag and close it up. To ensure that the bag is completely sealed, fold the top over twice. In the microwave, heat the bag for one minute and a half at the highest power setting. Cut the bag open with care, and then empty its contents into a large bowl or other container.
4. First, in a large mixing bowl, combine the butter and salt, then add the popcorn and toss to coat. Place some popcorn kernels on a baking sheet, and then put the sheet into the oven to make the popcorn.
5. Take the smoked meat from the grill after it has smoked for ten minutes. After serving, finish with a finishing sprinkling of parmesan. Enjoy!

Serving Suggestion: smoked herb popcorn with fruit juice

Attempt quinoa for a change!

Bacon Jam

Total Time: 45 Minutes

Portion: 2

Recommended pellets: Pecan

Ingredients:

• 7 slices Thick Cut Apple Smoked Bacon
• 3 Medium Onions
• 1/5 cup Balsamic Vinegar
• 1/5 cup Brown Sugar
• water as needed
• Salt and Pepper to taste

Direction:

1. Remove the onion's skin and cut it into extremely thin slices.
2. When bacon is cut very thinly, it tastes the best.
3. If you want your bacon to be well browned and have a little crunch to it, use a deep sauté pan and lay it on the pit boss grill when the heat is set to medium. Remove the pan from the heat source, pour off the fat, and keep aside 1 tablespoon of the liquid.
4. Combine the slices of bacon, brown sugar, balsamic vinegar, and water in a mixing bowl.
5. Cover and continue to cook over low heat for fifteen minutes, or until the onions have become more tender.
6. Remove the cover and continue stirring the onions often to prevent them from catching fire. If the amount of moisture falls too low, you may restore it by adding a few drops of water at a time.
7. Keep an eye on the onions, and if required, give them a little shake. To reduce the mixture to the consistency of jam, let for about one hour to pass.
8. If you put it in a container that seals well, you may keep it in the refrigerator for up to a week.

Smoked Cashews

Total Time: 1 Hour

Portion: 6

Recommended pellets: Hickory

Ingredients:

• 1 pound roasted, salted cashews

Directions:

1. Prepare the smoker by adding wood pellets into it. Close the grill's lid and preheat it to 120 degrees Fahrenheit.
2. On a baking sheet that has a rim, smoked the cashews for one hour while stirring them halfway through the process.
3. As soon as the cashews show signs of browning on the grill, remove them and store them in an airtight container so that they may be preserved for as long as possible.

Secret tip: Substitute any variety of nuts you like in this recipe. The wood-fired flavor works perfectly with any type. If using raw nuts, the time will need to be increased to about 4 hours because raw nuts must be cooked for this recipe to work. I tend to stick with roasted, salted nuts, as they take less time and typically have the right amount of salt.

Delicious Deviled Crab Appetizer

Total Time: 10 minutes

Portion: 30

Recommended pellets: Pecan

Ingredients:

- Cooking sprays, oils, and butters meant to prevent food from sticking.
- 16 ounces of lump crabmeat, big size
- 1 cup of divided panko breadcrumbs 1 cup of corn from a can, drained 12 cups of minced scallions, separated
- 1/4 cup mayonnaise 1 beaten egg 1 pinch salt
- One teaspoon of freshly ground black pepper
- Split 2 teaspoons of red pepper flakes Lemon juice

Directions:

1. Prepare the smoker by filling it up with wood pellets and turning it on. While maintaining the cover, bring the temperature up to 425 degrees Fahrenheit.

2. To make the crusts for the muffins, spray three mini muffin pans with cooking spray, divide the panko evenly among the cups, and then press it firmly into the bottoms and up the sides of 30 of the cups. (If you do not have enough pans, split the work among the available people.)

3. In a medium bowl, combine 14 cups of chopped scallions, 1 cup of chopped bell pepper, 1 cup of chopped crabmeat, 1/2 cup of mayonnaise, 1 egg, salt, pepper, and 1 teaspoon of cayenne pepper.

4. Place the mixture into the mini muffin pans, and then on top of each one, sprinkle the remaining half cup of breadcrumbs.

5. It is possible to smoke the meals for ten minutes with just a little amount of wood on the grill rack while the rack is covered.

6. In a small bowl, combine the remainder of the mayonnaise, the scallions, the cayenne pepper, and the lemon juice.

7. The crab cakes taste the best when they are served hot, and the sauce should be poured on top of them just before they are served.

Carne Asada Tacos

Cooking Time: 1 Hour

Portion: 3

Recommended pellets: Cherry

Ingredients:

- ½ tablespoon black pepper
- One tablespoon garlic powder
- Two lime, juiced
- One tablespoon salt
- 1 ½ lb. steak, skirt
- Eight tortilla

Direction:

1. Do you enjoy traditional carne asada street tacos? Throw a skirt steak on the pit boss grill and let the Smokey flavors take you to your favorite taco Tuesday joint.

2. Turn the grill to "smoke" and leave the lid open until a fire develops in the burn pot (3-7 minutes).

3. Preheat the pit boss grill to 400 degrees Fahrenheit. Cook the steaks for 4-8

minutes on one side then turn and cook for another 4-8 minutes on the other side.

4.   Remove the steaks from the grill and lay aside for 5-10 minutes, covered loosely with foil. The steaks may then be sliced into pieces and served with tortillas and any additional toppings desired.

Chapter 11: BAKED GOOD RECIPES

Smoked Pepperoni Pizza

Total Time: 2 hours 45 minutes.

Portion: 4

Recommended Pellet: Hickory

Ingredients:

- 1 lb. Italian sausage meat.
- ½ cup pepperoni slices.
- ¾ cup mozzarella cheese, grated.
- ½ cup green olives, sliced.
- ¾ cup pizza sauce.

Preparation:

1. Warm the smoker for 15 minutes with the lid closed at 250 degrees Fahrenheit (125 degrees Celsius).

2. To begin, mix the sausage meat with the olives well.

3. After that, roll the meat into a 10 inch by 10 inch square on parchment paper.

4. Next, place the pepperoni slices in the middle portion of the square.

5. Top it with the cheese and roll up the meat square.

6. Prepare the roll for smoking, and smoke it for 2 1/2 hours, or until the interior temperature reaches 165 degrees Fahrenheit (71 degrees Celsius).

7. Serve it with the pizza sauce.

Tip:

- You can even try adding bacon to the roll.

Whole meal bread

Total Time: 15 minutes for loaf

Portion: 3

Recommended pellets: Royal Oak

Ingredients:

- 750 grams of whole meal flour
- 2 teaspoons of salt
- a sachet of yeast
- 2 tablespoons of oil
- 1 teaspoon of brown sugar
- 500 ml of warm water
- 1 beaten egg

Directions:

1.   Put flour, yeast, and salt in a bowl and mix.

2.   Put the water, sugar, and oil in another bowl and mix well, then add them to the bowl with the flour.

3.   Start kneading with your hands and continue until you get a soft and malleable dough.

4.   Now put the dough on a lightly floured work surface and knead for another 10 minutes.

5.   Divide the dough into 3 parts and place them in three bread molds brushed with olive oil.

6.   Cover the molds with cling film and let them rise for 40 minutes.

7.   The Pit Boss must be warmed for 15 minutes at 482 degrees Fahrenheit with the lid closed, which should be completed after 40 minutes.

8.   After coating the bread with the beaten egg and putting it in the Pit Boss, bake it indirectly with the lid closed for 15 minutes.

9.   After 15 minutes, remove one loaf of bread and leave the other in the mold to complete baking.

10.   Before being cut, the bread must rest for 10 minutes.

Focaccia with onion and bacon

Total Time: 15 minutes

Portion: 4

Recommended pellets: hickory, cherry, apple

Ingredients:

- 250 grams of flour

- 5 grams of brewer's yeast

- 160 ml of water

- 1 small onion

- 100 grams of bacon cut into cubes

- 30 grams of grated Emmenthal

- Olive oil to taste

- Salt and pepper to taste

Directions:

1.   In a bowl, combine the salt and flour.

2.   Add yeast, vegetable oil, and water. Begin kneading the ingredients by hand, and continue until you have a smooth, lump-free dough.

3.   The dough must rise for one hour in a basin covered with a kitchen towel.

4.   While you wait, the onion must be peeled, rinsed, and sliced.

5.   2 minutes over medium heat in 1 tablespoon of oil, caramelize the onions.

6.   Three minutes later, add the bacon to the pan and saute it. After adding salt and pepper, turn off the heat.

7.   After the dough has rested for sixty minutes, turn it out onto a board dusted with flour.

8.   Roll out the dough with a rolling pin to create a thin layer of dough.

9.   Arrange the onion and bacon on one-half of the dough, taking care to leave a little margin from the edge.

10.   Fold the unseasoned pasta over the seasoned one and close the edges.

11.   Put the grated Emmenthal on the surface of the focaccia then let it rest for another 20 minutes at room temperature.

12.   Preheat the Pit Boss at 482 ° F for 15 minutes.

13.   Put the pizza stone to heat 10 minutes.

14. With the help of a pizza shovel, place the focaccia on the stone.

15. Cook with the lid closed for 15 minutes.

16. After 15 minutes, remove the focaccia from the barbecue and let it rest for 5 minutes.

17. Now cut it into slices and serve.

Potato focaccia with rosemary

Total Time: 20 minutes

Portion: 8

Recommended pellets: Apple Wood

Ingredients:

- 300 grams of flour

- 200 grams of potatoes

- 140 ml of warm water

- 1 teaspoon of brown sugar

- 7 grams of brewer's yeast

- Olive oil to taste

- Salt and pepper to taste

- 1 tablespoon of rosemary needles

Directions:

1. Start with the potatoes; wash them thoroughly under running water without peeling them.

2. Cook them for 25 minutes in plenty of boiling salted water.

3. Just cooked, drain, pass them under cold water and peel them.

4. Mash them with a potato masher and collect them in a bowl.

5. Add the flour, baking powder, 2 teaspoons of salt, sugar, and water.

6. Knead vigorously for at least 15 minutes until the mixture is soft.

7. Compact it with your hands and give it the usual shape of a ball. Cover with cling film and let it rise for 2 hours.

8. Preheat the Pit Boss at 464 ° F for 15 minutes.

9. Put on the pizza stone and let it heat up for 15 minutes.

10. Brush a round baking pan with olive oil and put the dough inside.

11. Roll it out with your hands and brush the surface with olive oil.

12. Sprinkle with a little salt and rosemary needles and put the baking pan on the pizza stone.

13. Close the lid and cook for 20 minutes.

14. Check the cooking and if the focaccia is golden brown, remove it from the barbecue; otherwise, continue cooking for another 5 minutes.

15. Just cooked, remove it from the barbecue and let it rest for 5 minutes.

16. After 5 minutes, cut it into 8 slices and serve.

Quiche with mushrooms, bacon and mozzarella

Total Time: 30 minutes

Portion: 8

Recommended pellets: cherry pellets

Ingredients:

- 1 roll of puff pastry

83

- 300 grams of mushrooms

- 2 mozzarella

- 100 grams of bacon cut into cubes

- 1 clove of garlic

- 100 ml of cooking cream

- 40 grams of grated Parmesan cheese

- 1 egg

- Salt and pepper to taste

- Olive oil to taste

Dircetions:

1.   Start by washing and drying the mushrooms and then cut them into slices.

2.   Peel and wash the garlic and then chop it.

3.   Put a tablespoon of oil in a non-stick pan, and as soon as it is hot, put the garlic to brown.

4.   Add the pancetta and brown it for 3 minutes.

5.   Add the mushrooms, season with salt and pepper, and cook for 10 minutes.

6.   Turn off and let them cool.

7.   Put the egg, the cooking cream, and the Parmesan in a bowl.

8.   Mix with a whisk until you get a homogeneous mixture.

9.   Put the mixture of mushrooms and bacon and mix again.

10.   Put the puff pastry in a round baking pan brushed with olive oil.

11.   Prick the bottom of the puff pastry with a fork and then put the filling inside.

12.   Preheat the Pit Boss with the lid closed for 15 minutes at 482 ° F.

13.   Place the baking dish in the center of the grill, cover, and cook for thirty minutes.

14.   As soon as it is cooked, remove it from the grill and let it rest for 10 minutes to enable the juices to settle.

15.   After 10 minutes, cut it into slices, put it on plates, and serve.

Chapter 12: DESSERT RECIPES

Apple Pie

Total Time: 30 minutes

Portion: 4 - 6

Recommended Pellet: Apple

Ingredients:

- ¼ cup of Sugar

- 4 Apples, sliced

- 1 tbsp. of Cornstarch

- 1 tsp. Cinnamon, ground

- 1 Pie Crust, refrigerated, softens in according to the Directions: on the box

- ½ cup of Peach preserves

Directions:

1. Preheat the grill to 375F with closed lid.

2. In a bowl, combine the cinnamon, cornstarch, sugar, and apples. Set aside.

3. Place the piecrust in a pie pan. Spread the preserves and then place the apples. Fold the crust slightly.

4. Place a pan on the grill (upside - down) so that you do not brill/bake the pie directly on Preferred Wood Pellet.

5. Cook 30 - 40 minutes. Once done, set aside to rest.

6. Serve and enjoy!

Chocolate Chip Cookies

Total Time: 30 minutes

Portion: 12

Recommended Pellet: Walnut, Hickory, Maple

Ingredients:

- 1 ½ c. chopped walnuts

- One t. vanilla

- Two c. chocolate chips

- One t. baking soda

- 2 ½ c. plain flour

- ½ t. salt

Directions:

1. Fill the smoker with wood pellets and start. Preheat your smoker with your lid closed until it reaches 350F.
2. Mix the baking soda, salt, and flour.
3. Cream the brown sugar, sugar, and butter. Mix in the vanilla and eggs until it comes together.
4. Slowly add the flour while continuing to beat.
5. Place aluminum foil onto grill. In aluminum foil, drop spoonfuls of dough and bake for 17 minutes.

White Chocolate Bread Pudding

Total Time: 1hr 15 minutes

Portion: 12

Recommended pellet: maple

Ingredients:

- 1 loaf French bread
- 4 cups Heavy Cream
- 3 Large Eggs
- 2 cups White Sugar
- 1 package White Chocolate morsels
- ¼ cup Melted Butter
- 2 teaspoons Vanilla
- 1 teaspoon Ground Nutmeg
- 1 teaspoon salt
- Bourbon White Chocolate Sauce
- 1 package White Chocolate morsels
- 1 cup Heavy Cream
- 2 tablespoons Melted Butter
- 2 tablespoons Bourbon
- ½ teaspoon Salt

Directions:

1. Get ready pellet smoker or any flame broil/smoker for cooking at 350°.

2. Tear French bread into little portions and spot in a massive bowl. Pour four cups of Heavy Cream over Bread and let sit for 30minutes.

3. Mix eggs, sugar, softened spread, and vanilla in a medium bowl. Include a package of white chocolate pieces and blend. Season with Nutmeg and Salt.

4. Pour egg combo over the splashed French bread and blend.

5. Pour the combination into a buttered 9 x 13 inch dish and put in smoker.

6. Cook for 60Secs or until bread pudding has set and the top is darker.

7. For the sauce: Melt margarine in a saucepot over medium warm temperature. Add whiskey and cook for 3 to 4 minutes until liquor is vanished and margarine is darkish-colored.

8. Include cream and heat to a mild stew. Take from the warmth and mix in white chocolate pieces a bit at a time continuously blending until it has softened. Season with a hint of salt and serve over bread pudding.

Coconut Chocolate Simple Brownies

Total Time: 25 minutes

Portion: 4 - 6

Recommended Pellet: hickory

Ingredients:

- 4 eggs
- 1 cup Cane Sugar
- ¾ cup of Coconut oil
- 4 oz. chocolate, chopped
- ½ tsp. of Sea salt
- ¼ cup cocoa powder, unsweetened
- ½ cup flour
- 4 oz. Chocolate chips

- 1 tsp. of Vanilla

Directions:

1.   Close the grill lid and preheat the grill to 350 degrees Fahrenheit.
2.   Butter and line a 9 by 9-inch baking sheet with parchment paper.
3.   In a bowl, combine the flour, cocoa powder, and salt. Mix well, then set aside.
4.   Chocolate and coconut oil may be combined in the microwave or a double boiler. Wait till it has cooled off.
5.   Add sugar, eggs, and vanilla essence to the batter. Whisking the ingredients will help them combine better.
6.   Combine with flour and a few chocolate chips. Incorporate the ingredients into a pan.
7.   On the grill should be placed the pot. Set the timer for 20 minutes and place the dish in the oven. For drier brownies, increase the baking time by 5 to 10 minutes.
8.   Let them cool before cutting.
9.   Cut the brownies into squares and serve.

Apple Crumble

Total Time: 1 hour and 30 minutes

Portion: 8

Recommended pellets: oak

Ingredients:

- 2 cups and 2 tablespoons flour, divided
- 1/2 cup shortening
- Pinch salt
- 1/4 cup cold water
- 8 cups apples, sliced into cubes
- 3 teaspoons lemon juice
- 1/2 teaspoon ground nutmeg
- 1 teaspoon apple butter seasoning
- 1/8 teaspoon ground cloves
- 1 teaspoon cinnamon
- 1/4 cup butter

Directions:

1.   Set your wood pellet grill to smoke.
2.   Preheat it to 350 degrees F.
3.   Mix 1 1/2 cups flour, shortening, and salt in a bowl until crumbly.
4.   Slowly add cold water. Mix gently.
5.   Refrigerate the dough for a minimum of twenty minutes.

The pot should be placed on the grill. Prepare for 20 minutes. If you want drier brownies, bake them for 5 to 10 minutes longer.

6.   Place the apples in a bowl.
7.   Toss in lemon juice. Take the dough out.
8.   Press into a pan.
9.   In a bowl, combine the 2 tablespoons flour, nutmeg, apple butter seasoning, ground cloves and cinnamon.
10.   Add this to the bowl with apples.
11.   Incorporate the butter and beat the mixture until it resembles coarse crumbs.
12.   Spread this on top of the dough.
13.   Bake for 1 hour.

Smoked Pumpkin Pie

Total Time: 50 Minutes

Portion: 8

Recommended pellets: cherry

Ingredients:

- 1tbsp cinnamon

- 1-1/2 tbsp pumpkin pie spice

- 15oz can pumpkin

- 14oz can sweetened condensed milk

- 2beaten eggs

- 1unbaked pie shell

- Topping: whipped cream

Directions:

1.   Preheat your smoker to 325F.

2.   Place a baking sheet, rimmed, on the smoker upside down, or use a cake pan.

3.   Combine all your ingredients in a bowl, except the pie shell, then pour the mixture into a pie crust.

4.   Place the pie on the baking sheet and smoke for about 50-60 minutes until a knife comes out clean when inserted. Make sure the center is set.

5.   Remove and cool for about 2 hours or refrigerate overnight.

6.   Serve with a whipped cream dollop and enjoy it!

Chapter 13: RUBS & SAUCES RECIPES

Bourbon Barbecue Sauce

Total Time: 40 minutes

Portion: 8-12

Recommended pellets: Hickory, Pecan, Cherrywood, Applewood

Ingredients:

- ½ onion (minced)
- ¾ cup bourbon whiskey
- 4 cloves garlic (minced)
- ½ teaspoon black pepper (ground)
- 2 cups ketchup
- 1/3 Cup cider vinegar
- ½ tablespoon salt
- ¼ cup tomato paste
- ½ cup packed brown sugar
- ¼ cup Worcestershire sauce
- 1/3 Teaspoons hot pepper sauce (or add as you see fit)

Directions:

1. Set your wood pellet smoker grill for indirect cooking.

2. Let the grill heat at 320 degrees Fahrenheit for 20 minutes with the lid closed.

3. Grab a large skillet, and add your garlic, whiskey, and onion. Let it all simmer for 20 minutes on your smoker grill. You're waiting for the onions to get translucent.

4. Toss in the salt, ground black pepper, tomato paste, ketchup, Worcestershire sauce, vinegar, brown sugar, and hot pepper sauce. Mix it all up.

5. Bring it all to a boil then drop the heat to 225 degrees Fahrenheit and then let it simmer for 20 minutes more.

6. If you like your sauce smooth, then use a strainer to extract it from the onions and stuff.

7. Enjoy this sauce with your barbecue meals!

Texas Style Coffee Mop Sauce

Total Time: 25 minutes

Portion: 8 to 12

Recommended pellets: apple wood, cherry wood, maple wood

Ingredients:

- 1 tablespoon sugar
- 1 cup Catsup
- ¼ cup butter
- ½ cup Worcestershire sauce
- 1 cup dark or strong coffee
- 1 tablespoon black pepper (fresh, coarse, ground)
- 1 tablespoon kosher salt

Directions:

1. Mix all your ingredients in a pot large enough to allow you to work without it spilling over.

2. Set up your smoker grill for direct cooking.

3.   Preheat your smoker grill to 350 degrees Fahrenheit for 15 minutes with the lid closed.

4.   Now simmer your ingredients on your smoker grill for 20 minutes. Allow it to thicken. Enjoy!

Beer Mopping Sauce

Total Time: 20 minutes

Portion: 8 to 12

Recommended pellets: flaked corn, pecan, apple, cherry wood chips

Ingredients:

- 12 ounces of beer
- ½ cup water
- ½ cup cider vinegar
- ½ cup canola or corn oil
- ½ onion (medium, chopped)
- 2 garlic cloves (minced)
- 1 tablespoon Worcestershire sauce
- 1 tablespoon brisket seasoning

Directions:

1.   Whisk your ingredients in a saucepan.

2.   Set up the grill for direct cooking.

3.   Let the grill heat at 350 degrees Fahrenheit for 15 minutes with the lid closed.

4.   Let your ingredients simmer on the grates until they come to a boil then lower the heat.

5.   Let it get nice and thick, and then take it off the grill, and let it cool.

6.   Best pellets: hickory

Carolina Mopping Sauce

Total Time: 5 minutes

Portion: 8 to 12

Recommended pellets: smoke wood chips

Ingredients:

- 1 cup cider vinegar
- 1 tablespoon hot sauce
- 1 tablespoon red pepper flakes
- 1 cup distilled white
- 1 teaspoon onion
- 1 teaspoon garlic
- 2 tablespoons brown sugar (packed)
- 1 teaspoon dry mustard
- ½ teaspoon salt
- ¼ teaspoon black pepper (ground)

Directions:

1.   Simply mix all your ingredients and then store in an air-tight fridge for a month.

2.   If you need more heat, just add some more red pepper flakes.

Smoked Tomato Cream Sauce

Total Time: 1 hour & 30 minutes

Portion: 2

Recommended pellets: hickory, applewood, and alder

Ingredient:

- 1 lb. beefsteak tomatoes, fresh and quartered

- 1-½ tbsp. olive oil

- Black pepper, freshly ground

- Salt, kosher

- ½ cup yellow onions, chopped

- 1 tbsp. tomato paste

- 2 tbsp. minced garlic

- Pinch cayenne

- ½ cup chicken stock

- ½ cup heavy cream

Directions:

1.   Toss tomatoes and 1 tbsp. oil in a bowl, mixing, then season with pepper and salt. Use a smoker rack to smoke the tomatoes for about 30 minutes. Take out, and save the tomato liquid for another use. Half a tablespoon of oil should be heated in a pan over medium heat.

2.   After the oil has heated, add the onion and sauté for another three to four minutes. Cook the tomato paste and garlic for one further minute. Cook for three to four minutes after adding the smoked tomatoes, cayenne, tomato juices, pepper, and salt. Repeated stirring is required.

3.   Toss in some chicken stock and simmer for 25 to 30 minutes. Repeated stirring is required. Puree the ingredients in a blender until completely smooth. Now, to separate the juices from the particles, press the mixture through a fine-mesh sieve. Move the sauce to a small saucepan and add the cream.

4.   Simmer for about 6 minutes on low to medium heat, stirring occasionally, until somewhat thickened. Spice things up with some salt and pepper. Keep heated and serve with risotto cakes.

Montreal Steak Rub

Total Time: 5 minutes

Portion: 1

Recommended pellets: Hickory, Almond

Ingredients:

- 2 tbsp. salt

- 2 tbsp. cracked black pepper

- 3 tbsp. paprika

- 2 tbsp. red pepper flakes

- 2 tbsp. coriander

- 1 tbsp. dill

- 1 tbsp. garlic powder

- 1 tbsp. onion powder

Directions:

1.   Simply place all ingredients into an airtight jar, stir well to combine, then close.

2.   Use within six months.

Smoked Mushroom Sauce

Total Time: 1 hour & 30 minutes

Portion: 4

Recommended pellets: Walnut, Hickory, Pecan

Ingredients:

- 1-quart chef mix mushrooms

- 2 tbsp. canola oil

- ¼ cup julienned shallots

- 2 tbsp. chopped garlic

- Salt and pepper to taste

- 1/3 cup alfasi cabernet sauvignon

- 1 cup beef stock

- 2 tbsp. margarine

Directions:

1.   Crumple four foil sheets into balls. Puncture multiple places in the foil pan then place mushrooms in the foil pan. Smoke in a pellet grill for about 30 minutes. Remove and cool.

2.   Heat canola oil in a pan, sauté, add shallots, and sauté until translucent. Add mushrooms and cook until supple and rendered down. Add garlic and season with pepper and salt. Cook until fragrant.

3.   Add beef stock and wine then cook for about 6-8 minutes over low heat. Adjust seasoning. Add margarine and stir until sauce is thickened and a nice sheen. Serve and enjoy!

Chapter 14: BONUS RECIPES (Thanksgiving day; Memorial day; Labor day; Father's day)

Thanksgiving day:

Whole Turkey

Total Time: 7 hours and 30 minutes

Portion: 10

Recommended pellets: alder

Ingredients:

- 1 frozen whole turkey, giblets removed, thawed
- 2 tablespoons orange zest
- 2 tablespoons chopped fresh parsley
- 1 teaspoon salt
- 2 tablespoons chopped fresh rosemary
- 1 teaspoon ground black pepper
- 2 tablespoons chopped fresh sage
- 1 cup butter, unsalted, softened, divided
- 2 tablespoons chopped fresh thyme
- ½ cup water
- 14.5-ounce chicken broth

Directions:

1. Turn on the smoker with the ash damper closed, then load the hopper with the dry pallets.
2. Prepare the smoker by setting the temperature to 180 degrees Fahrenheit and let it to heat for thirty minutes, or until the green light illuminates.
3. While the bird is cooking, use kitchen thread to tuck its wings underneath it.
4. Rub the turkey's inside and exterior with a mixture of 12 tablespoons of butter, fresh herbs (thyme, parsley, sage, orange zest, and rosemary), and salt and pepper.
5. To smoke a turkey, lay it breast-side up in a roasting pan, cover it with broth and water, add the remainder of the butter, and then place the pan with the lid on a smoker grill.
6. To achieve a well-cooked chicken, smoke it for 3 hours at 250 degrees Fahrenheit before raising the temperature to 350 degrees for another 4 hours, basting it every 30 minutes with the drippings except for the last hour.
7. After cooking, the turkey should rest for 20 minutes before to serving.
8. Carved to perfection, serve the turkey in bite-sized portions.

Turkey Meatballs

Total Time: 50 minutes

Portion: 8

Recommended pellets: Pecan

Ingredients:

- Turkey meat, weighed to within a 1/8th of a pound
- Breadcrumbs measuring half a cup
- 1 beaten egg
- Milk, 1/4 cup
- 1/2 an onion powdered
- Worcestershire Sauce, 1/4 Cup
- a pinch of garlic salt
- To taste, with salt and pepper
- One cup of cranberry preserves
- Orange marmalade, 1/2 cup
- A Half Cup Of Chicken Broth

Directions:

1. Combine the ground turkey, breadcrumbs, egg, milk, onion powder, Worcestershire sauce, garlic salt, salt, and pepper in a large mixing bowl.

2. Form meatballs from the mixture.

3. Warm up the grill for 15 minutes with the lid closed at 350 degrees Fahrenheit while using wood pellets as the fuel.

4. Add the turkey meatballs to a baking pan.

5. Turn on the grill and place the baking pan on it.

6. Cook for 20 minutes.

7. The remainder of the ingredients should be simmered for 10 minutes over medium heat in a pan.

8. Add the grilled meatballs to the pan.

9. Coat with the mixture.

10. Cook for 10 minutes.

11. Tips: You can add chili powder to the meatball mixture if you want spicy flavor.

Roasted Green Beans With Bacon

Total Time: 15 Minutes

Portion: 6

Recommended pellets: hickory

Ingredients:

- Green beans
- one pound of bacon cut into 4 pieces
- 4 tablespoons of extra-virgin olive oil,
- 2 minced cloves of garlic
- 1 teaspoon salt

Directions:

1. It is recommended that the temperature be set at 400 degrees. Your grill can accommodate a wide variety of pellets of your choosing. Put the lid back on and reheat it up in the oven for 15 minutes with the door closed.

2. Everything should be spread out in a single layer on a baking sheet.

3. Twenty minutes should be spent roasting the tray on the grill rack.

Smoked Cranberry Sauce

Total Time: 1 hour

Portion: 2

Recommended pellets: cherry, apple

Ingredients:

- 12 oz. bag cranberries
- 2 chunks ginger, quartered
- 1 cup apple cider
- 1 tbsp. honey whiskey
- 5.5 oz. fruit juice
- 1/8 tbsp. ground cloves
- 1/8 tbsp. cinnamon
- ½ orange zest
- ½ orange
- 1 tbsp. maple syrup
- 1 apple, diced and peeled
- ½ cup sugar
- ½ brown sugar

Directions:

1. Preheat your pellet grill to 375 F.

2. Place cranberries in a pan then add all other ingredients. Place the pan on the grill and cook for about 1 hour until cooked through.

3. Remove ginger pieces and squeeze juices from the orange into the sauce. Serve and enjoy!

Smoked Salted Caramel Apple Pie

Total Time: 30 minutes

Portion: 4-6

Recommended pellets: black cherry

Ingredients:

For the apple pie:

- One pastry (for double-crust pie)
- 6 Apples
- For the smoked, salted caramel:
- 1 cup brown sugar
- ¾ cup light corn syrup
- 6 tbsp. butter (unsalted, cut in pieces)
- 1 cup warm smoked cream
- 1 tsp. sea salt

Directions:

Grill Prep:

1. Fill a container with water and ice.

2. Grab a shallow, smaller pan, and then put in your cream. Take that smaller pan and place it in the large pan with ice and water.

3. Set this on your wood pellet smoker grill for 15 to 20 minutes.

4. For the caramel, mix your corn syrup and sugar in a saucepan, and then cook it all using medium heat. Be sure to stir every so often until the back of your spoon is coated and begins to turn copper.

5. Next, add the butter, salt, and smoked cream, and then stir.

6.   Get your pie crust, apples, and salted caramel. Put a pie crust on a pie plate and then fill it with slices of apples.

7.   Pour on the caramel next.

8.   Put the top crust over all of that and then crimp both crusts together to keep them locked in.

9.   Create a few slits in the top crust so the steam can be released as you bake.

10.   Brush with some cream or egg, and then sprinkle with sea salt and raw sugar.

On the Grill:

1.   Set up your wood pellet smoker grill for indirect cooking.

2.   Preheat your wood pellet smoker grill for 10 to 15 minutes at 375 degrees Fahrenheit, keeping the lid closed as soon as the fire gets started (should take 4 to 5 minutes, tops).

3.   Set the pie on your grill and then bake for 20 minutes.

4.   At the 20-minute mark, lower the heat to 325 degrees Fahrenheit, and then let it cook for 35 minutes more. You want the crust to be a nice golden brown, and the filling should be bubbly when it's ready.

5.   Take the pie off the grill and allow it to cool and rest.

6.   Serve with vanilla ice cream and enjoy!

Memorial day:

Cheesy Lamb Burgers

Total Time: 20 minutes.

Portion: 6

Recommended pellets: Hickory, Cherry, Applewood

Ingredients:

* Ground lamb weighing 2 pounds.
* Grated Parmigiano-Reggiano cheese equaling one cup.
* Add salt and freshly ground black pepper to taste.

Directions:

1. It is recommended that the grill be warmed for 15 minutes at a temperature of 425 degrees Fahrenheit with the lid closed.
2. Put everything in a bowl, and make sure it's well combined.
3. Create four patties with a thickness of three quarters of an inch using the ingredients.
4. Make an indentation in the center of each patty using your thumbs. The depression should be approximately three inches broad and one inch deep.
5. Cook the patties for six to eight minutes, making sure the depression side is facing down on the grill.
6. Continue to cook for an additional 8 to 10 minutes on the other side.

Roasted Hasselback Potatoes

Total Time: 30 Minutes

Portion: 6

Recommended pellets: Hickory

Ingredients:

* 6 large russet potatoes
* 1-pound bacon
* ½ cup butter
* Salt to taste
* 1 cup cheddar cheese
* 3 whole scallions, chopped

Directions:

1. Set the temperature to 350 degrees. Cook with the kind of wood pellets you like most. Put the cover on and heat for 15 minutes.

2. Place two wooden spoons on either side of the potato and slice the potato into thin strips without completely cutting through the potato.

3. Chop the bacon into small pieces and place in between the cracks or slices of the potatoes.

4. Place potatoes in a cast iron skillet. Top the potatoes with butter, salt, and cheddar cheese.

5. Place the skillet on the grill grate and cook for 30 minutes. Make sure to baste the potatoes with melted cheese 10 minutes before the cooking time ends.

Smoked Watermelon

Total Time: 45-90 Minutes

Portion: 5

Recommended pellets: hickory

Ingredients:

- 1 watermelon without seeds
- Wooden skewers
- Balsamic vinegar

Directions:

1. Remove the ends of little seedless watermelons.
2. Cube the watermelon to a 1 inch thickness. In a jar, watermelon cubes are arranged, and then a little quantity of vinegar is poured on top.
3. Start by preheating the smoker to 225 degrees Fahrenheit. The preheating of the smoker is not complete until wood chips and water are introduced.
4. Insert cubes onto the skewers.
5. 50 minutes in the smoker with the skewers. Cook.
6. The skewers must be extracted.

Labor day:

Lamb Chops

Cooking time: 10 minutes

Portion: 8

Recommended pellets: apple

Ingredients:

For the Lamb:

• 18 lamb chops lean 2 tablespoons Greek Freak seasoning

For the Mint Sauce:

• One teaspoon of chopped parsley
• Twelve onion slice
• 12 peeled cloves of garlic
• A tablespoon of mint, minced dry oregano, and a quarter teaspoon of oregano.
• An amount equal to one teaspoon of salt
• one-fourth teaspoon of ground black pepper
• Juice of a third of a lemon
• 1/4 liter olive oil

Directions:

1. Simply throw all of the ingredients in a food processor and pulse for one minute, or until the sauce is completely smooth. This will create the mint sauce.
2. After placing the lamb chops and a third of the mint sauce in a plastic bag, securing the bag, and inverting it will ensure that the meat is coated with the mint sauce. Allow the meat to marinade in the refrigerator for a minimum of half an hour.
3. Put some apple-flavored wood pellets into the pellet grill, turn it on using the control panel, set the temperature dial to smoke, or preheat the grill to 450 degrees Fahrenheit for at least 15 minutes.
4. After being drained and seasoned with Greek spice, lamb chops need to be roasted in the oven to get the best results.
5. After the grill has been heated and the cover has been removed, the lamb chops should be smoked for about 4–5 minutes on each side, or until they reach the desired doneness.
6. After the lamb chops have been baked for the desired amount of time, take them from the oven and arrange them on a tray to be served.

Grilled Pork Chops

Total Time: 4 hours & 10 Minutes

Portion: 6

Recommended pellets: Cherry Wood, Alder Wood, Hickory Wood

Ingredients:

• 6 pork chops, thickly cut
• BBQ rub

Directions:

1. Turn the grill up to 450 degrees.
2. Put a lot of barbeque rub on the pork chops. Cook the pork chops for 6 minutes on the grill, turning once, or until an instant-read thermometer registers 155 degrees Fahrenheit.
3. After grilling, take the food off the heat and let it rest for 10 minutes.
4. Enjoy.

Roasted Tuscan Thighs

Total Time: 1 hour

Portion: 4

Recommended pellets: Apple, Cedar

Ingredients:

• 8 chicken thighs, with bone, with skin

• 3 extra virgin olive oils with roasted garlic flavor

• 3 cups of Tuscan or Tuscan seasoning per thigh

Directions:

1. Wood pellets may be used to heat the smoker grill to 375 degrees Fahrenheit, the perfect temperature for indirect cooking.

2. Depending on the temperature of the grill, alter the roasting time from 40 to 60 minutes until the thickest part of the chicken thighs reaches 180 degrees Fahrenheit. The tenders from a Tuscan roast should rest for 15 minutes in a tent of loose foil.

Father's day:

Barbecued Shrimp

Total Time: 20 Minutes

Portion: 4

Recommended pellets: apple or cherry

Ingredients:

• Just under 2 ounces of shrimp
• 4 tablespoons of butter
• seafood seasoning sufficient for one dish

Directions:

1. For 30 minutes, immerse the wooden skewers in water.
2. Prepare the smoker by adding wood pellets into it.
3. Close the grill's cover and preheat it to 375 degrees Fahrenheit.
4. Place 4 to 5 shrimp on each skewer.
5. Rub olive oil all over the shrimp and season both sides of the skewers with the rub.
6. Laying the shrimp on skewers and placing them directly on the grill grates for 5 minutes on each side is a method for cooking shrimp. Remove the skewers from the heat and serve them immediately.

Grilled Steak with Mushroom Cream Sauce

Total Time: 1 hour & 25 minutes

Portion: 5

Recommended pellets: Maple

Ingredients:

• ½ cup of Dijon mustard

• 2 minced cloves of garlic

• 2 tablespoons of bourbon

• 1 tablespoon of Worcestershire sauce

• 4 beefsteak tenderloin

• 1 tablespoon of peppercorns

Others:

• Extra-virgin olive oil, 1 tablespoon
• 1 small onion, chopped
• 1 garlic clove, minced
• White wine, half a cup
• half a cup of chicken stock
• Sliced mushrooms, 16 ounces
• a quarter of a cup of full-fat cream
• To taste, with salt and pepper

Directions:

1. In a small mixing bowl, mustard, garlic, bourbon, and Worcestershire sauce should be blended.
2. The steak is coated with the mustard mixture by putting it in a Ziploc bag and vigorously shaking it. The steak requires roughly one hour of resting time.
3. Place the peppercorns, salt, and pepper in a small dish and combine them until they are uniformly distributed.
4. Remove the steak from the bag and massage it with the peppercorn mixture using clean hands.
5. Close the lid of your Wood Pellet Smoker and grill and warm it at 180 degrees Fahrenheit for fifteen minutes.
6. After placing the meat on the grill, smoke it for almost an hour. To cook a steak to an internal temperature of 130 degrees Fahrenheit, take it from the grill, increase the temperature to 350 degrees Fahrenheit, and cook for an additional 20 to 30 minutes.

7.   The sauce is prepared by heating a pan with oil and onions over a pellet grill for a few minutes.

8.   Garlic requires just one minute in the pan. After adding the mushrooms, cook them for a few minutes longer.

9.   Reduce the heat to a simmer and stir in the stock, wine, and seasonings to taste. Add the heavy cream and boil for a further 5–7 minutes.

10.   After thoroughly combining all ingredients, serve the steak with the sauce and relish..

Bacon and Sausage Bites

Total Time: 45 minutes

Portion: 2

Recommended Pellet: white oak

Ingredients:

- Smoked sausages - 1 pack
- Thick-cut bacon - 1 lb.
- Brown sugar - 2 cups

Directions:

1.   Slice 1/3 of the sausages and wrap them around small pieces of sausage. Use a toothpick to secure them.

2.   Line a baking tray with baking paper and place the small pieces of wrapped sausage on it.

3.   Sprinkle brown sugar on top.

4.   Preheat the pellet to 300 degrees.

5.   Keep the baking tray with the wrapped sausages inside for 30 minutes.

6.   Remove and let it stay outside for 15 minutes.

7.   Serve warm with a dip of your choice.

Chapter 15: DRINK RECIPES

Smoked Margarita

Total Time: 20 minutes;

Portion: 1

Recommended Pellets: Cherry

Ingredients:

- 12 Whole lime wedges, slit in center
- 1/2 Cup turbinado sugar
- 1 1/2 Cup Fresh Squeezed Lime Juice from Grilled Limes
- 3 Cup silver tequila
- 1 1/2 Cup Cointreau
- 3/4 Cup Smoked Simple Syrup, plus more to taste
- 1/2 Cup Bloody Mary Cocktail Salt
- lime wedge, for garnish

Directions:

1. When ready to cook, set the temperature of the Pit Boss to 500 ° F and preheat for 15 minutes, lid closed.

2. Halve the limes, dip in turbinado sugar and put flesh side down on the preheated grill.

3. 5 minutes of grilling or before you get a little char. Take the limes off the grill and juice them.

4. Using a pitcher to add lime juice, tequila, Cointreau and Smoked Simple Syrup. Stir to blend.

5. Place Bloody Mary Cocktail Salt just wide enough to match the glass rim in a low-sided dish.

6. Run the lime round each rim of the bottle, dip the rim in the salt and fill the glass with ice.

7. Pour in the margarita mixture and garnish with a slice of lime. Enjoy!

Healthy Coffee Smoothie

Total Time: 10 minutes

Portion: 1

Recommended pellets: none

Ingredients:

- 1 tablespoon chia seeds
- 2 cups strongly brewed coffee, chilled
- 1-ounce Macadamia Nuts
- 1-2 packets Stevia, optional
- 1 tablespoon MCT oil

Direction:

1. Use a blender to thoroughly combine all of the ingredients until they form a creamy consistency.
2. When blended at a high speed, the mixture becomes completely smooth.
3. Cheers to excellent drinking!

Strawberry And Rhubarb Smoothie

Total Time: 7 minutes

Portion: 1

Recommended pellets: none

Ingredients

- 1 rhubarb stalk, chopped
- 1 cup fresh strawberries, sliced
- ½ cup plain Greek strawberries

- Pinch of ground cinnamon
- 3 ice cubes

Direction:

1. In a small saucepan, boil water over high heat.
2. Once boiling, add the rhubarb and simmer for three minutes.
3. The contents must be drained and well mixed.
4. Add strawberries, honey, yogurt, cinnamon and pulse mixture until smooth
5. Add ice cubes and blend until thick and has no lumps
6. Pour into a glass and enjoy chilled

Delicious Pineapple And Coconut Milk Smoothie

Total Time: 5 minutes

Portion: 2

Recommended pellets: none

Ingredients

- ¼ cup pineapple, frozen
- ¾ cup of coconut milk

Direction:

1. Place all of the ingredients listed on the list into a blender, and process them until they are completely smooth.
2. After everything has been mixed together, pour the smoothie into a big glass, and serve it chilled.

Paloma Cocktail

Total Time: 5 minutes;

Portion: 3

Recommended Pellets: Oak

Ingredients:

- 2 grapefruit, halved
- As Needed Smoked Simple Syrup
- 5 Stick cinnamon
- 1 1/2 Ounce reposado tequila
- 1/2 Ounce lime juice
- 1/2 Ounce Smoked Simple Syrup
- grilled lime, for garnish
- cinnamon stick, for garnish

Directions:

1. Set the Pit Boss temperature to 350 ° F when ready to cook and preheat, the lid closed for 15 minutes.

2. Grapefruit Juice Grilled: Split 2 grapefruits in half. Place each grapefruit half with a cinnamon stick and glaze with Smoked Simple Syrup. Place it on the grill and cook for 20 minutes or until the edges begin to burn and grill marks are obtained. Remove and let cool from the sun.

3. Squeeze and strain the juice after the grapefruits have cooled. The juice can yield 10 to 12 ounces.

4. Put the tequila, lime juice, Smoked Simple Syrup and 2 ounces of grilled grapefruit juice in a mixing glass.

5. Shake and add ice. Strain in an old-fashioned glass over ice.

6. To garnish, add a grilled lime slice and a cinnamon stick.

Hi,

The time has come for the conclusion of the book! I hope this book was able to give you the right information to answer the questions you were looking for answers to. In case the answer is yes, I kindly ask you to leave an honest and dispassionate review saying what you liked or what you learned from the following reading.

This would mean a lot to me, and help me disseminate this information and thus help other people like you.

Should this book not meet your expectations, please do not hesitate to contact me at this email: gallopublishingltd@gmail.com .. That way, we will have a chance to talk about it and find a solution. Also, your feedback will allow me to improve my product and ensure a better experience for the next buyer.

Thank you very much and have a good day ☺

CONCLUSION

Thank you for trusting me and buying this cookbook. I hope this book may have solved the problems you bought it for, and I sincerely hope I have been helpful.

As I said, I wrote this book intending to lead an aspiring pitmaster to be the best in his or her neighborhood.

The one thing I would like to mention is that practice will make you the best pit master. People often think it is enough to have a set of recipes and a good guide to master a pellet grill like an expert. Still, unfortunately, that is not the case as in anything to become the best, you need to apply and practice a lot.

This book, by doing so, can be a real accelerator to achieving your pitmaster goals.

Now enough of the talk, get involved and start smoking your meat for bbq.

Made in United States
Orlando, FL
11 February 2023

29782077R00059